STRATEGY & TACTICS OF LAND WARFARE

CHARTWELL
BOOKS INC.

Edited by **Will Fowler**

Published by Chartwell Books Inc,
A division of Book Sales, Inc,
110 Enterprise Avenue,
Secaucus, New Jersey 07094

Printed in Great Britain

ISBN 0 85685 504 9

CONTENTS

LAND
WARFARE

Men and Terrain

General Ulysses S. Grant in his headquarters during the American Civil War.

Strategy in war is primarily concerned with the formulation of policy. This involves the selection of war aims, the establishment, maintenance or dropping of alliances on a political level, and the application of resources to achieve military objectives. The tactics of a war, on the other hand, are the methods of fighting and manoeuvre employed to secure the immediate objective that is in itself part of the strategic plan. In land fighting, tactics are normally associated with regimental (and below) level tasks, although this can depend on circumstances. The dividing line between strategy and tactics can become extremely blurred.

The strategy of war has, on the whole, not changed radically through the ages, but tactics, with their greater dependence on methods and means have. Glubb Pasha, the British officer who commanded the Arab Legion noted that: While weapons and tactics may change, terrain and men do not. It could, of course, be argued that terrain can and does change and that man himself has altered over the ages, but one cannot really quarrel with the statement: that ground over which action is fought and the motives, fears and hopes of the combatants have remained essentially unchanged, although weapons and their tactical and strategic deployment have altered as a result of human ingenuity. Indeed, advances in civilization could cynically be identified with man's growing capacity to kill ever increasing numbers of people by single, less intensive efforts, and primitiveness with man's inability to kill except at very close range or in hand-to-hand conflict.

The physical nature of war has altered radically within the last 150 years, for technological advances in weaponry have produced massive changes not only in the concept of the battlefield itself, but have also led to a widening of the conflict to include the civilian population on a scale never before realized. A soldier who had fought with Caesar in Gaul, for instance, would have had very little difficulty in recognizing his counterpart in Napoleon's Grand Armée; each fought shoulder-to-shoulder with his comrades in a close-quarter battle. His commanders, too, differed little in their approach, with their reliance on infantry, cavalry and supporting arms. Transplant those soldiers to World War I, however, and neither they nor their commanders would have recognized the battlefield, nor indeed what the commanders were attempting. By World War II, battlefield dispersal had become even more marked, although both Caesar and Napoleon may have been more confident with the strategic direction.

Traditionally armies were organized into four basic groups: infantry, cavalry, artillery and the supporting arms, particularly the commissariat. The three 'teeth arms' – infantry, cavalry, artillery – had their own part to play, but in battle also attempted to operate together to attain victory. The backbone was the infantry, soldiers operating on foot with their own personal weapons, a firearm and bayonet. Their role was the defeat of the enemy infantry by superior firepower or close quarter action, the conquest and occupation of ground. In addition, they gave close support to the artillery and relied on the guns to destroy physically or morally the enemy infantry, artillery and defensive positions (e.g. fortresses). The cavalry existed to fulfil three basic tasks: to reconnoitre and locate the enemy and pass accurate information back to the commander, to provide a screen behind which the main part of the army could advance or retreat without harrassment by the enemy and, finally, to provide shock on the battlefield in the form of the charge. Secondary functions included the picking off of enemy stragglers and the scouring the battlefield of a defeated enemy.

The ability of the three teeth arms to carry out their traditional roles, however, has undergone considerable change during the last century or so, even though the basic definitions remain unaltered.

The ability of commanders to realize a tactical objective has been greatly hampered by developments, particularly in weaponry, that in themselves have ultimately produced strategic stalemate. Whereas, traditionally, commanders attempted in battle either to split an enemy front in the centre, or to turn either or both flanks, or to encircle an enemy and hence achieve the annihilation of all or a part of its army, by the latter part of the nineteenth century, their ability to do so was largely prevented by technological developments. Tactical success could not be turned into decisive strategic success because the cost of that tactical success was too great in lives and time for its rapid exploitation. This happened mainly because offensive strategic development could be offset by a more rapid defensive deployment by an enemy using exactly the same means and tactics. The climax of this situation came about during the First World War and the deadlock of that war necessitated a fresh tactical approach that restored strategic and tactical mobility.

Historians have generally seen the evolution of modern warfare as stemming from the great political and technological changes brought about by the

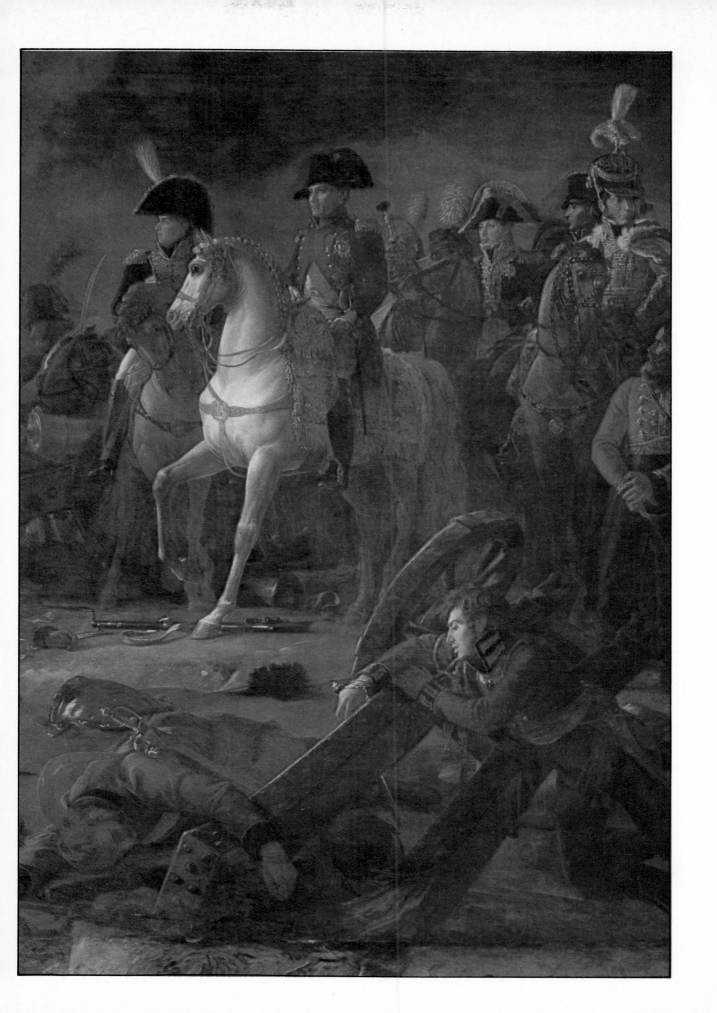

A Union 12-pounder field gun battery preparing to fire during the American Civil War. This was the last war in which muzzle-loading smoothbore artillery predominated on both sides.

French Revolution and Napoleonic Wars (1792–1815), and the Industrial Revolution of the nineteenth century. Certainly the French wars introduced into conflict an element of totality – of national as distinct from dynastic struggle, of victory as opposed to marginal territorial gains – that had been absent from Europe since the end of the wars of religion. The wars in defence of the Revolution had necessitated popular participation in the form of the *levee en masse* to withstand the seasoned professional armies of monarchical Europe. The French wars drained all countries and after Waterloo most countries would have preferred to revert to small professional armies but for certain developments. After her defeat in 1806 Prussia had introduced conscription, the obligation of compulsory military service for men between 17 and 50 years of age. By this means the concept of a standing army based upon conscription in time of peace was introduced.

And ultimately the other major countries of mainland Europe followed Prussia's example.

The consequences of such changes were bound to be profound. With larger armies the demand placed upon society itself – financial, industrial, moral – proportionately increased; politically wars became less manageable in that the mobilization of reserves (the essential prerequisite of a nation in arms) inevitably lessened the chances of avoiding wars and also made less likely the prospect of halting, limiting or ending a war once it had begun because of the emotionalism and sacrifice inherent in a national recourse to arms. In their turn larger armies implied a more ponderous tactical deployment plus the prospect of prolonging wars since the availability of reserves could hold off threatened breakthroughs and deny an enemy any decisive initial success. Such was the influence of the growth in the size of armies, made possible by the synthesis of two

6

conditions: the first the political will on the part of states to bear the cost and second the development of railways.

Rail was first used for troop transportation in a Prussian exercise in 1846; but the first operational use took place in Italy during the Franco-Austrian war of 1859. Railways simplified the problems of strategic manoeuvrability, supply and the evacuation of wounded, but they were also inflexible and imposed rigidity on their users. While troops arrived at their destination in good condition they were tied to their railhead for supplies and their mobility in the field remained the same as it had been since time began – the speed of animal or human legs. The greater number of troops available meant greater congestion and greater problems of command and control. Thus railways were double edged in effect: they conferred greater strategic mobility (to both sides) but hampered political con-

siderations (by the need to mobilize) and reduced strategic and tactical mobility by putting forces into the field too large to be effectively wielded and tactically slower than an enemy's strategic deployment capability. Moreover, if the growing ability to concentrate manpower in a given area more quickly than hitherto was lessening tactical mobility, technological developments, particularly in the fields of chemistry and metallurgy, were adding to the problem. And both problems were compounded by an understandable human failure to appreciate to the full the impact of these changes.

Traditionally the imprecision of weapons dictated the need for close-range fighting between massed infantry (backed by artillery and supported by cavalry) since volume of fire was more important than individual marksmanship. Because of the cumbersome nature of their weapons, the infantry had to load and fire while standing. New weapons, however, altered this situation.

Breech loading, rapid-firing rifles for both infantry and artillery opened effective killing ranges, to the immediate embarrassment of a boot-to-boot cavalry charge. The 50-100m (50-100 yard) ranges of smooth-bore muskets increased fivefold by mid-century, while rapid-firing rifles meant a greater volume of fire could be delivered from a soldier in the prone position. In Prussian hands such rifles proved their worth in Denmark (1864) and Austria (1866) while the French in the Chassepot procured a superior weapon that only their strategic and tactical incompetence negated in the Franco-Prussian war of 1870–71. (Repeating rifles, fed by a magazine, were introduced during the American Civil War though they took some twenty years for general adoption in Europe.) Likewise, in artillery, steel replaced bronze and iron, breech-loading rifles smooth-bore muzzle-loaders, with the result that the ranges of Napoleon's time quadrupled. Moreover quickly firing guns mounted on recoil-absorbing carriages enabled gunners to dispense with re-adjustment after firing, while improved explosives and propellants enabled employment of smaller calibres that by definition retained mobility for the artillery.

These developments among others opened battlefield ranges and upset the balance between the three teeth arms. Infantry firepower could shatter a cavalry charge long before the cavalry could close to effective range and an infantry assault could be similarly broken up by artillery before it closed the target. But infantry, entrenched or behind earthworks, had a large degree of protection against artillery. The American Civil War amply demonstrated that entrenched infantry, backed by artillery, could inflict debilitating losses on an attacker – irrespective of colour of uniform. The power of the defence had for the moment outstripped that of the offence. The lessons that might have been drawn went largely unheeded in Europe, in part because three of the most important wars – in the United States, in South Africa and in Manchuria – were far away and could be dismissed as having little relevance to Europe. Von Moltke the Elder, the Chief of the German General Staff, contemptuously dismissed the notion that American events had lessons for Europe; the British were simply not considered as a military factor; and Manchuria and the Russian experience could be put down to extreme local factors. Certain concessions to reality were made however: the Russian experience in 1877 outside Constantinople showed the necessity of digging in under fire because of the heavy losses incurred in frontal assault on even field fortifications: infantry tactics necessitated a thinning of an advancing wave into an extended skirmishing line with the fire fight being won at ranges between 400 and 600m (400 and 600 yards). Infantry advanced by waves in depth until fire supremacy had been achieved before the final bayonet assault was launched from ranges of about 100m (100 yards). The British cavalry for a short time after South Africa carried a carbine (a short barrelled rifle) but subsequently reverted to lance and sabre as did other armies who experimented with machine guns to add to the power of their recce forces. But for the most part the lessons were missed: the Polish banker Ivan Bloch, predicted in 1911 that a future major war would be a terrible war of attrition in

Right: The Maxim gun was the first effective machine-gun to be used in action. It is seen here with a British crew during the Boer War in South Africa. Of all weapons in the 20th century the machine-gun has had the greatest impact on land and air warfare. Below: An 18-pounder with its British crew during the First World War.

which defence would predominate. Such a war would be a lingering trial of strength, involving all the physical and moral resources of the combatants, only to be resolved when the strain proved too great for one of the sides. Most people tended to dismiss such observations. The reality of war was distant in Europe by the turn of the century: nationalist propaganda, in all countries, in stressing what were regarded as national traits, came to place moral factors as the supreme consideration in the pursuit of victory. Elan and the imposition of moral authority, a heady and romantic concoction assumed a greater importance than detailed consideration of the effectiveness of defensive machine guns. The process of disillusionment was to take four bloody years to complete.

Trench Deadlock

The trenches in World War I: a British sergeant peers over the parapet while his comrades 'stand down'.

A British tank of the First World War. Tanks were a war winning weapon but like so many new weapons their operators were often unaware of their full potential. Poor battle drills, unsuitable areas of deployment and mechanical failure dogged the first attacks, but by the end of the war men and machines were used with great success.

Even before World War I began, it was apparent that the rate of technological advance was exceeding man's ability to understand it – and nowhere was that more starkly illustrated than in the military. The men who led the armies of all the combatants in World War I had been fashioned by a quite different era and they were unable to cope with a total war which produced such tactical innovations as trench warfare, the use of aircraft and the introduction of the tank – all of which destroyed the traditional concept of battle procedure. In fairness to them, it must be said that matters were simply beyond their competence and they had to deal with problems for which their experience and training had not equipped them, though in all honesty, it must be admitted that few displayed much imagination in tackling them. Nevertheless, they were the best available at the time and in certain theatres – Mesopotamia, Palestine, the Balkans – some acquitted themselves well; even on the Eastern Front certain Russian generals, such as Brusilov, and Conrad of Austro-Hungary displayed abilities that were not attended by commensurate success. But these, in the end, were not the decisive fronts. It was the Western Front, a line which ran through Belgium, France and Germany from the English Channel to Switzerland, that was so vital it is still virtually synonymous with World War I. A picture that is painted of shattered trees, shell-holes filled with scum-covered, cordite-reeking water, being drunk to the dregs by decomposing corpses, a murdered strip of nature hundreds of miles long that engulfed the greatest hopes of Europe: World War I evokes deadlock, stalemate. This is not false but neither is it wholly accurate. In the opening weeks of the war, in the last eight months of the war in the West, on fronts other than in the West (particularly in Russia and the Balkans) there was movement, much movement, that seemed to be discounted or ignored.

In 1918 the Central Powers (Austro-Hungary, Germany, Turkey and Bulgaria) were defeated by the Allies (primarily France, Belgium, Britain and the USA) when the former became convinced that despite their sacrifices in four years of war they could not secure through a military victory gains that could justify their losses. By the time this conviction became general the vaunted German offensives of the spring and summer, designed to secure victory, had been held and thrown back. The German Army, while still intact and on foreign soil at nearly every point, was in retreat in the West and facing defeat if not in 1918 then

certainly in 1919. The Central Powers had been held together by hopes of German victory: they were broken, morally, when that victory proved elusive. They were beaten not because of superior Allied strategy or tactics but because their means of waging war, physical and psychological, had been exhausted. War had become siege warfare conducted by nations: it had become total and in doing so the military effort had become only a part of the strength – albeit possibly the most important single ingredient – that could not survive when hope had gone and these other ingredients, financial, industrial, economic, agricultural, psychological had been bankrupted. By the time of the armistice, stark famine stalked central Europe; epidemics raged; domestic heating was virtually non-existant. The Central Powers broke as a result of the cumulative strain from two sources that brought the Allies their victory: the superior geographical position of the Allies isolated them from the outside world, thus severing the trade in food and raw materials that could have sustained them, and secondly, the increasing industrial and human resources the Allies could bring to bear on the battlefield. In the end Britain and France almost broke before the Germans; but for the Americans they might have. But for all that, victory went to the side with the greater pool of killable manpower and superior economic resources.

That such a debilitating struggle had to be endured – that the Allies could not win more economically and the Germans not win at all – was the result of strategic failure and tactical stalemate on both sides. Neither side, either in its opening strategic deployment and manoeuvre or in its subsequent tactical undertakings, could impose its will on the enemy. The essential problem – at least for the Allies – was tactical for most of the war. Once trench warfare established itself, the superiority of defence over attack, as Bloch foresaw, meant that even though a defender's front might be broken, the attacker – hampered by losses, exhaustion and the problem of moving supplies and reinforcements into a breach – could not prevent the defence resealing the break in the front by the timely disposal of reserves, brought up by rail. This was the essential problem that all commanders, irrespective of nationality, faced in the war: the momentum of an assault based on human capability could not be sustained in the face of the strategic mobility conferred by railways on the defender.

That such a situation had arisen was the result of the

failure of both sides to achieve a decisive outcome in the opening weeks of the war. In part, these failures stemmed from human frailty and incompetence, in part from the lack of realism on the part of the war plans themselves, in part from insuperable tactical problems and in part from the impracticability of forcing a result given the growth of armies and a nation's durability.

Under the terms of the Schlieffen Plan (the German plan of campaign for a war against both France and Russia), the Germans stood on the defence in the East and on their left flank in the West, while four armies struck through Belgium, Luxembourg and Northern France to try to encircle and then annihilate the French field armies in eastern France against the anvil formed by their left flank. This was to be achieved in six weeks – the time between the start and completion of

Russian mobilization – with the German Army then entraining to deal with the Tsarist threat. The French plan for the invasion and clearing of German-occupied Alsace-Lorraine was torn to shreds; the Russian plan for the invasion and clearing of Eastern Prussia similarly fell to pieces; and the Austro-Hungarians scarcely had any worthwhile plans. But it was the failure of the Schlieffen Plan that really decided the nature of the war. As the Germans marched into France, barely delayed by the greatest fortress system in Europe at Liège that was destroyed by howitzers, they were checked by Anglo-French thrusts on their right flank from Paris and from the front at the Marne. A steadier nerve might have saved the day had the Germans tried to envelope the Marne thrust between their Ist and IInd Armies, but in fact they were pushed

back to the Aisne – a line of exhaustion for all three armies. The Schlieffen Plan failed mainly because it was too ambitious. It set for its soldiers (many of whom were reserves) the task of marching and fighting some 600 miles in a line of advance that took them across a whole series of river barriers running across the line of march and then, at the end of a tenuous line of communication served only by horse-drawn transport and exposed to attack on their unguarded flanks, fight a battle against an enemy not necessarily shaken by previous defeat. Moreover the Germans had no answer to the problem of Paris since they lacked the strength and time to take it; nor did they have an answer to the French advantage of lateral and radial railways to redeploy to meet an invasion limited by the speed and endurance of feet.

Thus the front stabilized along the Aisne and the south when the French Ist and IInd Armies managed to hold to the Verdun-Toul and Epinal-Belfort fortress lines after their disastrous defeat in Lorraine. (This attack, characterized by colour and bravery rather than any appreciation of military reality, had seen the French infantry in blue jackets and red trousers and the cavalry in breast plates and plumes attacking en masse behind bands and flags as if nothing had happened in 99 years.) As the front stabilized and neither side achieved a rupture of the enemy line, both sought the traditional strategic and tactical recourse – the turning of the open flank to the north in an effort to envelope the enemy flank. But with both sides attempting this simultaneously outflanking proved elusive and the sea was reached before either side gained the initiative. Once on the sea the front line solidified.

On the Eastern Front devastating success attended the initial Russian assault on the ramshackle Austro-Hungarian armies around Lemberg, but a premature move against the German positions was launched in East Prussia. This was attempted in order to clear the right flank preparatory to a thrust from Russian Poland towards Berlin but the attack by two armies designed to encircle the German army in the region was very badly scouted and even more ineptly co-ordinated. By masterly improvisation the Germans were able to use their central position and excellent rail system in the area to deal with the separated and diverging Russian armies in turn. The Russian Army was annihilated at Tannenberg, the French Army routed at the Masurian Lakes. But in the east, given the great distances and space and the lack of any major strategic objectives for which the Russians would have to fight or against which they could be trapped, the Germans lacked the means of securing a speedy and decisive success. Despite the demands of the Western Front the Germans in time were able to push the Russians out of the industrialized Baltic coast, Poland and Western Russia, inflicting unheard of losses on the Russian Army until in 1917 the Imperial structure collapsed. Russian victories over Turkey and Austria-Hungary (nations even less industrialized than herself) availed her nothing in her conflict with her industrial superior, Germany. Her overall lack of industry and loss of many of the great centres she had, the disruption of her railways and food distribution centres, her lack of ports, her weak social system ensured that with defeat Russia slithered into revolutionary chaos (as did Austria-Hungary and, to a lesser extent, Turkey). By this time, however, the

Left: A British 18-pounder, unsuitable for trench warfare and no protection against the first armoured attacks. Right: A German officer stands by his dramatically painted tank, his chain mail mask is a protection against shell splinters. Below: A German tank. The Germans were slower to adopt the armoured fighting vehicle in the First World War, but made up for this during the Second.

German opportunity for victory had passed. Strategically, she had never fully committed herself to forcing the issue by concentrating either in the West or the East, although with the enfeeblement of Russia she was able to redeploy to the West. But by that time the ultimate defeat had been secured, by her exhaustion, the arrival of the Americans and the tenacity of the British defence, when the Germans launched their offensive in the spring of 1918.

Strategy, for the British and the French, was largely determined by two considerations: Firstly, there was the belief that Germany could only be beaten by defeating her armies in the field; secondly, there was the inescapable reality of the German Army deep inside France itself. When fighting on one's own territory military logic cannot have the final say. Thus while attempts to outflank Germany were considered and implemented by the strategic use of exterior lines of communication in such theatres as the Dardanelles, Salonika, Palestine and Mesopotamia, the Western allies of necessity always found in the Western Front the main theatre for their offensive operations. Having an enemy on home territory the French (and their allies) had to attack. The Germans, for the most part, stood on the defence in the West, making only a minor

An Austrian howitzer in travelling position. These guns destroyed the Belgian forts with their heavy shells at the beginning of the First World War.

attack at Ypres in 1915, a major assault that quickly mushroomed uncontrollably at Verdun in 1916 and the final spring/summer assaults of 1918.

At the end of 1914 neither side fully appreciated the permanency of trench warfare. Wishful thinking convinced many that, with the spring, extra artillery, infantry and determination, the front could be breached and fluid fighting restored. Mobility on any scale did not come to the Western Front until 1918 when the British found themselves in retreat. Although many attempts were made to secure a permanent breach, none succeeded. The initial tactical response to the deadlock tended to be attempts by artillery to blast a way through the enemy position. Given the power of infantry firepower in defence, the attackers sought to provide greater artillery support for the infantry; for the British in particular, battles were seen as progressive advances under a series of detailed artillery fire plans that would either smash through or progressively weaken the enemy to the point when collapse would occur under the strain of the next attack. At Neuve Chapelle in 1915 the British attack opened with a short but intensive artillery assault, but on too narrow a front for an adequate breach to be effected. While initial objectives and the mastery of the first German trenches were being achieved liaison between infantry and artillery collapsed. The artillery was not therefore able to switch to fresh targets effectively, and command of units engaged by commanders virtually ceased to exist. The technology and techniques of the day were not adequate to cope with control of battle.

The second such assault at Aubers in May 1915 was even less successful even though artillery was more plentiful and used in a creeping barrage ahead of the advancing infantry.

During the course of the war British attacks opened by artillery bombardments increased in intensity and duration though after August 1918 they reverted, with success, to short duration bombardment. The extreme length of duration – deemed necessary to cut barbed wire defences and knock out known machine gun positions – in fact proved counter-productive. High explosive cratered the ground, making advance more difficult; at Ypres in 1917 advance was all but impossible because the fire destroyed the drainage system of the low lying area. Such bombardments also telegraphed intentions to the enemy, enabling him to deploy his reinforcements close enough to prevent a breach or to counter-attack but out of range of the initial assault. Moreover, the Germans evolved a defensive system in depth. Thick barbed wire defences were deployed in some areas while breast works in places 10m (30 feet) deep were equipped with underground shelters where troops could escape the worst of the artillery bombardment. On accosions these shelters could house a full battalion and be used as jumping off points for the assault. The Germans also thinned out their forces in the front line with the major part of their strength in the second or third trench lines: wherever possible these lines were sited on the reverse slope of a hill away from direct artillery observation.

Such defensive arrangements all but negated any tactical innovation, and certainly invalidated any attempt simply to blast a way through by artillery assault. Even the creeping barrage – designed to keep down the heads of the defenders until the infantry reached their position and to prevent the forward

deployment of the reserves by the defence – could not secure an economical advantage, while the damage to terrain by shell fire has already been noted. There was another type of shell that had the supreme advantage that it left the ground largely intact, at the same time having a wider area effect of quite long duration: the gas shell. Properly used – en masse and with ingredients against which the defender had no protection – gas might have produced tactical success leading to strategic success, but the German use of chlorine at Ypres in 1915 and phosgene at Verdun failed because of their faulty tactical employment. The frontages on which the chemicals were used were too narrow and at Verdun the Germans failed to risk all on phosgene and instead, after knocking out most of the French artillery, reverted to high explosives, thereby allowing the French to recover in time to meet the assault. Attacking troops, moreover, showed some understandable reluctance to move too closely into infected areas. From being a potentially war-winning weapon gas was relegated to being an additional endurance for the already over-laden infantry.

Infantry, weapons and tactics also altered considerably during the course of the war. Just as the shovel proved as essential as the rifle to the infantryman, trench warfare demanded the use of grenades, revolvers, pistols and nailed clubs for restricted close quarter fighting. Such fighting demanded – and produced – light weapons with high rates of fire (machine pistol) and weapons capable of clearing strong points (the flame thrower). Tactically it was left to the Germans to provide innovations. In the opening assault at Verdun in February 1916 the Germans employed infiltration tactics whereby assaulting infantry dispensed with any notion of an advancing skirmishing line and, operating in small groups utilizing cover and shell holes, infil-

trated a defensive position. As later refined in the 1918 assaults these tactics, based on covering fire to pin the enemy while the attacking force moved to the flank to carry out the destruction of the target, sought to exploit gaps in the defence. Attacking units were trained not to tackle points of resistance but to try to break through to the enemy artillery, leaving unreduced positions in their rear for the attention of follow-up units. Emphasis was placed on speed and momentum and such formations – known as storm troops – were equipped with grenades, light machine guns, light trench mortars and flame-throwers. The follow-up units (battle units) were more heavily equipped in that they had sections of artillery and trench mortars, plus engineers and supply troops. Their task was to reduce the points the initial wave left and to hold ground against the inevitable counter-attack, but they were also expected to take over the advance on storm troop exhaustion and to exploit enemy weaknesses. If the battle units failed to reduce the positions, these were to be left to heavier units with larger artillery following in the wake. The whole emphasis of these tactics was on speed and exploitation – trying to fight in the gaps where the enemy was not: and with reserves being fed into the points of least resistance, rather than the most stubborn.

The employment of these tactics – backed by meticulous artillery preparation to ensure surprise – by the Germans in their assault of March 1918 met with some local success. The British Fifth Army was all but destroyed on the Somme and a maximum penetration achieved; on May 27 the Germans advanced from their start lines on the Chemin des Dames. But tactical success was dearly bought: in the northern sector of the Fifth Army where mist did not hamper defence, ingenuity and bravery availed the attackers nothing. Caught in the open the infantry were cut down as

Right: A British soldier on guard in a captured German trench. His comrade is asleep wrapped in a ground sheet cape. Below: The terror of the trenches, a German sniper with an NCO spotting with binoculars, looks for a suitable target. Sniping needed patience and a ruthless temperament.

effectively as had they been in column: infantry itself could not provide a break through. Exhaustion, too narrow frontages of break through, the inevitability of a flanking machine gun pegging back the wings of the assault, the problem of getting the reserves to the right place at the right time to exploit a situation efficiently were insuperable tactical barriers. Strategically, there were other factors. However fast the storm troopers moved it was still with the speed of feet: defenders could move (strategically) by rail. They could throw down units in front of the advance to buy time to secure a rear defence line with fresh, unshaken troops. Any advance, moreover, left an numerically and psychologically weakened force holding a longer front and a tract of wrecked ground, across which it had to be supplied.

The only possible way a breach could have been opened and maintained would have been through some form of mechanized weapon. Such a weapon could have been an aircraft of sufficient endurance and bomb load to wreak havoc with a defender's communications and thereby exhaust and disorganize reserves. Alternatively, a land weapon of sufficient mechanical reliability, range and speed to take it through a defended zone into open country could also have provided the key. Technology of the day could not provide such reliable machines,

but it did provide the machines themselves, and their performance could only improve.

In its initial employment the tank was not cast in a role of deep penetration. It was used to crush barbed wire defences and assist the infantry in overcoming the enemy defence lines. At Cambrai (November 1917), after tanks had floundered on the Somme (1916) for want of numbers and at Ypres (1917) similarly, in the mud, the British Tank Corps drew up elaborate tactics to ensure infantry/armour co-ordination in order to open and maintain a breach. The attack was difficult

An infantry assault in World War I; a British officer leads his men 'over the top' from their front line trenches.

because the sector of attack was one of the strongest defensive positions in the German line and the trenches were too wide for the tanks to cross. The latter problem was overcome by deploying sections of three tanks each topped by a large fascine of brushwood. The lead tank was to crush the barbed wire and on reaching the enemy line move to the left and shoot up the enemy infantry; the left tank of the 'main body' was to move to the trench, drop its fascine and then cross, moving left to assist the process of trench clearing; the remaining tank was to cross the fascine and moved to the second trench line, drop its fascine and thus allow the original lead tank to move to the third line, fascine still unused. Thus it was hoped that a systematic clearing of trenches could be achieved without many infantry losses. Infantry were deployed, a platoon to each tank, following close behind in single file. One platoon was committed to marking routes through the wire, another the clearing of points of resistance, the last the holding of captured trenches. Behind this force came specialized tanks, some with supplies, others with grappling hooks intended to tear open the wire defences and thus allow cavalry egress because the cavalry was, hopefully, the means of deep penetration.

Cambrai did not succeed in making and sustaining the breach and indeed the battle, which began very well for the British, petered out indecisively. Responsibility for this largely rests on certain of the commanders involved but there is no ignoring the fact that the tanks were not adequate enough to make the break. At Cambrai 474 tanks were committed: 195 were intact at the end of the day though only 65 had been lost to enemy action. At Amiens on August 8, 1918 only 145 tanks were available for action after one day of fighting from an initial strength of 508. Most tanks were out of action because of mechanical problems: crews, too, were utterly exhausted by action in temperatures of 40°C (100°F) and badly affected by cordite and petrol (gasolene) fumes. Had more tanks been available in either of these actions for the second day, a breakthrough may have been achieved. The cavalry amply demonstrated its inability to exploit a breach but there was the prospect of light tanks and armoured cars filling this role. At Amiens 'Whippets' (light tanks capable of 13 kms/hr) and armoured cars more capable of getting into the German defences and savaging

supply columns headquarters and reserves were employed. This was a foretaste of what could happen once numbers and reliability could be assured, speeds raised and communications improved – but in World War I technology could not reach such levels.

Nevertheless, while the strategic and tactical deadlock of the war had necessitated a fresh tactical approach but had failed to provide one, the developments had provided the ingredients for mobile war in future. The tank, new infantry tactics and improved artillery techniques indicated immediate evolvement toward new concepts in land warfare. In addition Verdun (February-December 1916), showed that an army could be supplied solely by road transport if a railway was not available; the Battle of the Marne (1914) showed that an army could be moved strategically by motor transport if necessary. Admittedly in 1914 the distances involved were not great and at Verdun the front was mainly fixed, but the points were not invalidated for these reasons. Given the primitiveness and paucity of motor transport, the French achievements on these occasions were little short of miraculous. Moreover, aircraft emerged as a promising method of interdiction – the severing of the enemy's communications with a threatened area. In this role they could act as long-range artillery, the effectiveness of which was bound to grow as bomb loads increased. Larger loads also opened the possibility of using aircraft to supply units in the advance to growing effect; the British in fact dropped supplies by air to their forces on the Somme in August 1918. And before that they had already used aircraft for a similar purpose when, in one of the most imaginative (and underhand) coups of the war, prior to the start of the third battle for Gaza in 1917, they had dropped cigarettes and safe passes to the British lines on the Turkish positions. The cigarettes contained opium, a fact believed to be not unrelated to the relatively light losses incurred in the attack. The whole of the elaborate deception and security measures effected in this battle proved devastatingly effective and a stark contrast to most operations on the Western Front.

The legacy of World War I provided all the combatants with food for thought. All were agreed that a future war could never be fought in the manner of 1914–1918.

Triumph and Defeat

U.S Marines hunch behind a Browning water cooled machine-gun during the invasion of a Japanese held island in the Second World War.

In the search for a fresh tactical concept that could restore battlefield mobility after World War I, the British took the lead and retained it until the mid-thirties. Even before the end of the war one of the leading personalities in the Tank Corps, Major J. F. C. Fuller, produced a plan of campaign (usually simply called Plan 1919) that, when modified and circulated, caused intense debate. Fuller envisaged an attack on a ninety-mile front – against an enemy forewarned in order to bring more of his forces into the battle area for the purpose of ensuring their destruction. The plan was to use concentrations of medium tanks to sweep through the defensive zones to attack headquarters in the primary defensive zone and thereafter to fan out to attack other headquarters and areas of concentration and communication. The aim was to destroy the nervous system of the enemy, to deny him the means of tactical response. In this, the contribution of air power in a systematic interdiction role against supply and road centres was vital. For the land side of the operation Fuller envisaged some 2400 medium tanks for the assault. With the defender slipping into chaos as a result of his flanks being pierced and the medium tanks wrecking his lines of command and control, frontal assault by some 2592 heavy tanks, motorized infantry and artillery would be pushed through into the second tactical zone, thus accentuating the disintegration of the defence and leaving the enemy open to defeat.

Leaving aside the twin points that Germany sued for peace and thus avoided the fate Fuller had planned for her, and that the medium tanks did not fulfil their design specifications, Plan 1919 was imaginative and contentious. Equally when Fuller suggested that a new division could have twelve infantry battalions, each with a tank company, four battalions of horse-drawn and two companies of mechanized medium artillery and a mixed brigade of two cavalry and one armoured battalions, there were many traditionalists who opposed him. The greatest deterrent to adoption of his ideas, however, was the cut-back in the armed services after the war, of money and with it initiative and enthusiasm. It was not until 1927 that experiments were conducted with armoured forces on the scale and in the manner foreseen by Fuller. By that time, however, he had made a convert of an influential military correspondent, Captain B. H. Liddell Hart. The latter had devised a concept of infantry attack along a whole front to seek out the enemy weak spots and then erupt through them in 'an expanding torrent.' Fuller convinced Liddell Hart that infantry could not overcome tanks and that only tanks could provide the speed necessary for such a concept to have any chance of success. Liddell Hart was a far more tactful exponent of this concept than the prickly, abrasive Fuller though it was Fuller's stock that stood the higher among such people as de Gaulle in France and Guderian in Germany – two of many strategists outside Britain who carefully followed British writings and developments at this time.

The experiments of 1927 proved quite satisfactory for the armoured formations, but the forces established for such trials suffered from continual disbanding and re-establishing until 1934 when the tanks were set up on a permanent basis. By that time, moreover, British tanks led the world in communicating through radio sets, and the 1931 trials introduced for the first time a tank formation being effectively and immediately controlled by a single man, via radio. This was of vital importance since it would allow a very rapid reaction to events, such as a swift shift of force and direction of attack, and thus would fully utilize assets of mobility and shock both to exploit and to counter-attack.

Such developments tended to pass the French by. For France, security meant safety against defeat, not the prevention of war. She was secure against defeat through her alliances – with Belgium, Poland, Czechoslovakia and Russia and her understandings with Rumania and Yugoslavia – and through her overwhelming superiority over Germany by virtue of the numerical size and reputation of her army, particularly the infantry. Politically and strategically, however, she could never resolve the question of whether her alliances and understandings were sources of aid or commitments to be honoured. The ambiguity became apparent in the thirties as Hitler increasingly demonstrated that France's alliance system worked just as long as there were no threats to it. Strategy cannot be divorced from political will and in the twenties and thirties the French were victims of sapped and ever weakening determination. The full extent of her cripplingly high losses in World War I were increasingly felt, and she came to be dominated by two considerations: firstly, military theory stressed that the decisive arm in battle was the infantry, with the result that tank development and experimentation were geared to infantry tactics in the World War I manner. (As a result French tank evolution, though technically

French heavy artillery in a field position on the Maginot Line. Though they had tanks and aircraft as well as mobile artillery, the French were convinced that, following First World War experience, defence would produce more casualties to the enemy than attack. This left them open to any aggressive moves by the Germans.

sophisticated and novel in many ways, tended to be far slower and more limited than in other countries.) Secondly, France was hypnotized by the way in which the great Verdun fortresses had resisted months of attack and had held the German assault in 1916. In the thirties, convinced of the power of defence over attack and determined not to expose their manpower to the conditions of World War I ever again, the French applied themselves to building a system of permanent defences against which the Germans could batter themselves into exhaustion. The result was the Maginot Line a masterpiece of military engineering as far as it went – which was not far enough. The Line consisted of subterranean positions where units could live, exercise, feed, be hospitalized and fight in air-conditioned surroundings. Ground approaches to the Line from the enemy side were covered with obstacles and bunkers with uninterrupted fields of fire. These positions backed by massive gun emplacements and observation posts and the individual positions, were sited in order to assure mutual support from similar flanking emplacements. Though the Maginot Line was emulated (and in some places even surpassed) by the Czechs in the Sudetanland and the Soviets in the area between the Baltic and the Pripet Marshes, neither the Czechs nor the Soviets came to regard their defensive positions in the same manner as the French. The true aim of fortresses, the provision of time for the defender and the release of large formations for other under-takings, came to be relegated by the French to minor considerations when set against the feeling of security engendered by the line itself. In building the Maginot Line the French implicitly abandoned her eastern allies and any pretence of offensive action, even though the French Army manual of 1939 laid stress upon offensive action. This, however, could not undo the years of complacency and in any case envisaged an offensive strictly along World War I lines, namely a slow, deliberate advance by armour and infantry in mutual support under overwhelming artillery cover.

The Soviet Union, one might have imagined, would have been in the vanguard of change, given the nature of her revolutionary government, but in fact while she did experiment in the inter-war period her military doctrines were ultimately old-fashioned and conventional. Soviet strategic problems in the defence of the USSR against a western attack were immense. The Pripet Marshes split any attacking force but also divided the defending Red Army into two quite

separate wings. Since these were served by different rail systems, covered different but equally important areas – Moscow and Leningrad in the north, the Ukraine and Donetz in the south – and since there was no means of rapid or easy movement between the two sectors, there was little real opportunity for close co-operation between the two wings of the defence. For the most part Soviet strategic plans involved a light defensive stance in the north – backed after 1936 by the Stalin Line which, however, was never continuous – and deployment in strength in the south, ready, if all went well, for offensive operations into the Balkans. The whole problem was made worse by the huge frontages: almost by definition the great distances involved meant that they could not be strong everywhere and that the fronts had to have gaps. The Soviets did envisage aggressive action and by 1941 had thirty-nine tank divisions, but these were not grouped together but diluted in support of the infantry though separate from the latter who had their own tank and artillery units. The Soviet posture was thus that of the

traditional Russian steamroller, updated with modern equipment. There was much evidence to support such deployment. In Spain, the Soviets had supported the Republic and had seen balanced forces of infantry, armour and artillery exert consistent pressure on defensive positions to the point that the defence in all cases broke – most notably at Bilbao and on the Ebro. In actions when tanks operated without direct infantry and artillery support – particularly in exploitation – little success had been achieved. In the bloody encounter with the Japanese in August 1939 at Khalkin Ghol in Mongolia it was the same tactical combination – plus a lack of squeamishness about casualties – that brought the Red Army victory, just as it did in the 1939–40 Winter War against Finland. While such tactics proved adequate in these circumstances they proved totally inadequate in the encounter with the one nation that based an offensive doctrine on the developments in armoured warfare that had taken place after World War I. That country was Germany.

German doctrine, strategically, was characterized by

ruthless and vehement action conducted at great pace against an enemy's command and communications system. It aimed, through overwhelming concentration of force, particularly armour, to penetrate an enemy front and then to encircle and annihilate a surrounded enemy before he had time either to withdraw or mount a counter-attack. This form of warfare, called after its German name *Blitzkrieg* (lightning war), was based on the writings of Fuller and Liddell Hart but it had been left to a small group of enthusiasts in the German Army and the demonic genius of Hitler to overcome the prejudices and reservations of most of the German Army for its general adoption. *Blitzkrieg* envisaged a broad frontal attack in order that the enemy front should be gripped, thereby ensuring that contact could not be broken in order to launch counter-moves. With the enemy's attention held, the main blow(s) would fall on a relatively narrow frontage by concentrated armour and motorized forces. The leading German armour exponent, Heinz Guderian, stressed the need for a division to be built around the tank, not around the infantry: the division in the breakthrough had to move

at the pace of the fastest with the infantry keeping up, not with the tanks held back by lagging foot-soldiers. To this end he conceived a medium battle tank that possessed 'armour sufficient to protect it against the mass of enemy anti-tank weapons, a higher speed and greater cruising range than the infantry escort tank, and an armament of machine guns and cannon up to 75mm.' The tanks were to break through and to be immediately supported by motorized infantry whose task was manyfold – to mop up remaining enemy positions within the attacking area, to harden the flanks of the breakthrough in order to provide 'hard-shoulders' that could defeat a counter-attack and to move forward to exploit the success of the tanks. The motorized forces included specialist engineers – for bridging, demolition and, of course, for use of flame-throwers – but were also backed by mobile anti-tank guns and artillery. Some of these were towed by vehicles but the ideal form was tracked self-propelled guns. In practice the Germans had to use a combination of medium and heavy anti-tank guns, and tanks themselves, to defend vulnerable flanks and as a defensive

The German PzKw IV which was the workhorse of the armoured divisions. Early marks were in action in 1939 and 1940 and it was still fighting at the end of the war.

screen to take the impact of an enemy armoured attack. The most famous of the guns used in this role was the celebrated 88mm gun, originally designed as an anti-aircraft weapon.

The problem of shaking an enemy defensive position, physically and morally, had been the traditional role of the artillery. But as has been recounted, heavy artillery assault sacrificed surprise in timing and direction of attack, as well as impeding progress through breaking up the ground. The solution to this problem lay in the tactical use of air power against an enemy field force and position. In addition air power was used to paralyze the enemy's field forces by concentrating on his airfields and aircraft (in order to secure air supremacy), his road and rail centres, concentration of reserves and identified headquarters. The object was to prevent or to delay the enemy's redeployment of reserves to the threatened sector of the front, forcing the enemy to feed in his forces piecemeal and in poor order, if they arrived at all. The whole emphasis of action both on the ground and in the air was to delay the intervention of enemy anti-tank guns and tanks in the area of breakthrough except under conditions of utmost favour for the attacker. A further function of air power Guderian envisaged to be the use of parachute forces to secure important objectives – such as bridges – in the path of an armoured advance.

When Guderian was formulating his ideas (which he expounded in his book *Achtung – Panzer*) Germany did not have the means even to attempt such notions. Hitler and technology, however, were at hand to provide the opportunity. Guderian secured command of one of Germany's first three panzer regiments and became Chief of Armoured Troops on the General Staff. Under his guidance the panzer divisions were formed that, after the 'dry-runs' in the occupations of Austria and Czechoslovakia, tore the gallant but hopelessly equipped Poles to pieces in September 1939. The same panzer divisions, operating en masse to secure the very maximum advantage from their fire power and shock effect, ripped apart the French Army in May 1940 and brought about the collapse of the Belgian, British, Dutch and French armies in a six week campaign. In 1941 they were to overrun Yugoslavia and Greece before being lured eastwards to the unconquered steppes of the only country left in Europe not already subdued but capable of posing a serious threat – the Soviet Union.

By the time of the German attack on the USSR one major change had taken place in the panzer arm that was symptomatic of the progressive disease in the German Army – the increasing of units by the dilution of their strength. The Germans literally doubled the number of panzer divisions for their attack on the Soviet Union but this was achieved only by halving the strength of divisions. The new divisions contained between 150 and 200 tanks but with the extra staffs and back-up needed for indigenous units. In 1941 a panzer division had one panzer regiment with only two battalions (six divisions had three battalions in their panzer regiment): the battalions had one medium and two light companies. The divisions had two motorized

regiments, each of two battalions, a motor cycle regiment (mainly for reconnaissance) and a motorized artillery regiment of four battalions, one of which was an anti-aircraft battalion, equipped with the 88mm gun. As long as the Luftwaffe enjoyed air supremacy this weapon was usually deployed in an anti-tank role.

Nevertheless despite the reduction in strength the panzer divisions smashed their way into and through the Soviet defensive positions with little difficulty; it was only in the vast distances of the steppes that total victory eluded them. The Soviets had the space in which to retreat and bring up fresh units, trading space for time. France and Britain in 1940 had not had this space and had had to fight where they stood.

The 8.8-cm Flak was one of the great guns of the Second World War. It had been designed as an anti-aircraft gun, but its high velocity and flat trajectory made it a very effective anti-tank gun.

Moreoever they had lost not because they had fewer and poorer tanks than the Germans – indeed, on the contrary, the Western democracies had more tanks and they were in many ways superior to those deployed by the Germans. In the battles of 1940 and in the early engagements in the Soviet Union in 1941, the enemies of Germany lost because they were wedded to an inferior tactical doctrine and because they lacked the brilliance, elan and superior training of the Germans.

Blitzkrieg

A German soldier attacks an observation position during training on captured stretches of the Maginot Line.

Rommel, 'the Desert Fox', during an impromptu briefing in the chill of a morning in North Africa. Rommel demonstrated that even with limited resources, tactical flare and nerve could take an army from defeat to near triumph. His faults were a desire to lead from the front and, like a Napoleonic general, be seen where the main action was being fought.

The Second World War contained two separate wars – one fought on land in and around Europe, the other on sea around mainland Asia and the western and central Pacific oceans. In the end the Axis powers of Germany, Italy and Japan were defeated by the combined efforts of the world's great industrial and financial power (the USA), the world's most populous state (China), the world's great land power (the USSR), and the world's great Empire (Britain), plus a whole host of lesser countries. What is so astonishing is not the final defeat of the Axis powers (who were supported only by Finland, Hungary, Rumania, Bulgaria, Thailand and a motley collection of quisling states) but that they came so close to achieving victory – a glance at a map of Axis conquests in June 1942 reveals staggering success. Yet behind the conquests, the Germans and Japanese lacked the manpower, industry, transport and oil needed to bring their efforts to a victorious climax. As long as the Allies could evade defeat – and the British just managed to do this during 1940–43, the Soviet Union came to within measurable distance of utter ruin both in 1941 and 1942 – the superior economic, financial and industrial resources of the Allies were bound to bring victory in the end. For the Allies the war was one of attrition and the cost was enormous. The great killing matches of World War I on the Western Front were repeated on an even greater scale, not by the British, French and Americans but in Europe on the Russian Front, in the Far East in China, and at sea. The Soviets lost some 22 million people;

the Chinese some 14 millions. The cost in treasure was equally prodigal and the ruination of Europe and many areas of the Far East was virtually total.

The major factor in the extent of German and Japanese success lay in the twin facts that as aggressors they possessed the strategic initiative and that their gains prior to the outbreak of general war (1939 in Europe and 1941 in the Far East) had left them in positions of decided physical and moral superiority. The Allies had to fight for the strategic initiative and, in the case of Germany, it was not until 1943 that such initiative was wrested from her. And it was not until that same year that the high watermark of Japanese conquest began to ebb decisively.

German strategy in World War II was dominated by a desire not to become engaged in a long drawn-out campaign of the kind that had so drained her in blood and morale in 1918. Hitler, just as he had in the cases of Austria and Czechoslovakia, rejected the notion of a two-front war and sought instead to wage short wars, economical in manpower and minimal in disruption of the economy. He tried to tackle his enemies singly, picking them off one by one. He did not anticipate that Britain and France would declare war in 1939 over Poland because he thought that the non-aggression pact with the Soviet Union would lead the democracies to accept the *fait accompli* tamely. The destruction of Poland was no great problem for the Germans. She was indefensible in any strategic sense since she was surrounded on three sides by Germany: it was from East Prussia in the north and from Silesia and occupied Czechoslovakia in the south that the panzer columns erupted into Poland, the two arms of the pincer aiming to sweep behind Warsaw to achieve the encirclement and annihilation of the Polish field armies. (The aim of every German *blitzkrieg* attack was not a city but the enemy field forces.) In the case of Poland the battle was scarcely a contest. Totally outclassed in the air, the Poles were exposed to pulverizing air attack from the start. JU-87 Stuka dive-bomber aircraft, operating as precision artillery, pounded defensive positions and fortifications. Polish cavalry charged tanks with a predictability matched only by their commitment and bravery. The campaign was sharp, quick and brutal while the French, as Hitler had foreseen, undertook no offensive action to aid their hapless ally. Indeed the French, given their estimate that the Poles could offer a six-month resistance to the Germans, were as surprised by the ease of the German victory as were some of the Germans themselves.

The turn of the Western Allies was to follow in May 1940, though only after Denmark and Norway had been invaded in a daring and imaginative use of sea power. Though operating in the face of superior force, the combination of audacity and first blow brought the Germans an immediate advantage that ultimately proved decisive. In fact the Germans, who took severe naval losses in the Norwegian campaign, came perilously close to defeat and were saved more by the fumblings and mistakes of the democracies than by their own efforts. At this stage of the war the Western democracies were relatively pacific; they were not seeking to secure the strategic initiative. Granted that the prospects of alliance with the Soviet Union were non-existent and that the smaller states of eastern Europe were not prepared to embrace the western cause, the British and French were still prepared to stand on the defence, waiting for their strength to be built up. In May 1940 the British Army in France numbered ten divisions; in September 1940 it was to have been brought up to thirty-nine divisions. Only when the British and French had drawn on the full strength of their empires were they prepared to contemplate the offensive; until such time they were prepared to wait upon events.

Hitler could not afford to wait. He could not afford to let the balance of power shift remorselessly against him. In 1940 his armies were equal in size to the combined armies of the four major western European states, though Germany had the built-in advantage of unity of command and none of the lack of standardization that plagued the democracies. Only in the air did the Germans possess superiority of numbers and quality (3200 to 1800): in tanks they were outnumbered by about 2500 to 3000 and their artillery had 7710 pieces against the French total of 11,700. Time would only add to this imbalance. The Germans were therefore forced to take the initiative. In formulating their plan of attack they gauged Anglo-French reactions exactly. By attacking all along the Western Front and invading Belgium, Luxembourg and the Netherlands with a force of just over twenty-nine divisions (three of which were armoured, two being earmarked for subsequent transfer), they estimated that the Anglo-French field armies along the Franco-Belgian border would be lured into Belgium and southern Holland and there pinned by the two invading German armies. The main German thrust – in the form of a three army (forty-five divisions) assault – was to fall in the centre with the

seven armoured divisions concentrated for a blow on a forty-five mile front through the Ardennes to the Meuse between Dinant and Sedan. The main blow was to fall on Sedan, the very pivot of the Anglo-French manoeuvre into the Low Countries, and was to be delivered, appropriately enough, by Guderian's XIX Panzer Corps. The nineteen German divisions in the south were not intended to demonstrate the strength of the Maginot Line.

Strategically the plan was nearly perfect, aiming as it did to smash a decisive breach in the Allied line in the very centre, thereby allowing the encirclement of the trapped field armies. It was audacious in that a breakthrough to the Channel from Sedan – a place evocative enough for both Germany and France – left an exposed flank of some 200 miles across the front of the French Army. It was brilliant in the calculated risk of passing the bulk of the armour through a narrow congested area poorly served by roads and with good defensive positions. The weakness of the plan lay in its objectives once the breakthrough at Sedan had been made. There was no provision for exploitation of success either with regard to the occupation of France or the reduction of Britain. But the plan itself worked. The French Army was ripped into two on the Meuse within five days; the Channel was reached on May 25 – fifteen days after the battle began. The British Army plus some 100,000 French were able to escape from Dunkirk – largely because of German strategic timidity in forcing the panzers on in an area that had such an ominous reputation from World War I – but there was no escape for the others. The Dutch surrendered late in May, as did the Belgians. France was forced to sue for an armistice by June 22 (effective on the 25th). German losses amounted to 27,000 killed, 110,000 wounded and some 18,000 missing. Allied losses were estimated at 2.3 millions of whom about 1.9 million were prisoners.

On the European mainland Germany had no rival, given her understanding with the USSR, but her ally, Italy, brought about a crisis in the Balkans (already an area of conflicting interests between Germany and the Soviets) as a result of her ill-considered assault on Greece in October 1940. The Italian debacle produced a German intervention in the spring of 1941, with the result that Yugoslavia was annihilated in a nine-day campaign and Greece overrun. Following the occupation of Greece the Germans attempted a unique operation – strategic conquest by air in the form of a parachute invasion of Crete. The operation involved the

seizure and holding of an airhead on the island and the rapid reinforcement of the parachutists by sea and by air. This was very different from the type of operation that the Germans' single parachute division had been used to. In the Netherlands in 1940 and on the Corinth Canal in April 1941 they had been used as Guderian had wished, in front of an armoured advance. The battle for Crete was very finely balanced. Jumping from the slow and vulnerable JU-52s, the Germans took losses in the air and there was much confusion on the ground but they were able to take and hold Maleme, as much by good fortune and British error as their own efforts, and this proved decisive. The relentlessness of the Luftwaffe (the British had no air cover worth the mention), and the persistence of the German elite parachute and mountain troops, decided the issue. Nevertheless German losses were severe and they were never again able to launch such an operation.

For Hitler, however, Greece, Crete and indeed the whole of the Mediterranean area were diversions from the decisive theatre. But he could not ignore either the political or military realities of the Italian alliance and Italy's disastrous operations in North Africa, 1940–41. Such was the Italian situation that Germany had to intervene. Similarly, though on the reverse side of the coin, the British in fighting in North Africa had no strategic choice. Expelled from mainland Europe and

with no allies and no possibility of regaining a foothold on the continent, they had to fight where they were in land contact with the enemy, and only in Africa was there such contact. The indefensible Italian possessions in East Africa were quickly conquered; thus the British were involved in operation in the North African desert for the very good reason that there were no other areas where they could fight. Initially, they prospered against an Italian Army that was hopelessly ill-equipped, poorly officered and of very low morale. Few Italians enthused about the German alliance; even fewer were prepared to die for Mussolini. In December 1940 a 30,000 strong British force under the command of Major General Richard O'Connor began a raid against Italian forward positions at Sidi Barrani inside Egypt. Tactically the operation was characterized by sheer audacity (since the Italian armies in Egypt and Libya totalled 250,000 men) and the maximum use of security and surprise. The approach to contact involved night marches and lying up in the open between, and slightly in front of, the Italian positions. The attack was directed against the Italian centre, using exactly the same tactics as *blitzkrieg* – armour with motorized infantry, and mobile artillery acting with close air support. The Italians, taken by surprise, broke and in doing so lost any hope of rescuing something from the debacle. They were forced into one of the most difficult of military

Left: German troops in Russia. The vast distances and poor roads, as well as an inexhaustible supply of men, made the Russians an enemy who could not be defeated in three months like some smaller, western European armies. Below: British gunners with a howitzer in North Africa. The Desert war was one uncomplicated by civilians, towns and partisans and became the nearest thing to a 'gentleman's war'.

operations, to stand while in retreat and in contact with an aggressive enemy. They found no place to turn and fight, such was the relentless fury of British harrassment. As the Italians retreated through Derna they sought safety along the coast road, but O'Connor divided his dwindling forces and sent part of them on the landside of the Jebel Akhdar to reach Beda Fomm just before they arrived. Encirclement was complete, and at an overall cost of less than 2000 casualties the British destroyed ten Italian divisions, took 170,000 prisoners and captured 400 tanks and 850 guns – one of the most remarkable feats of arms in history. Total strategic success was denied the British, however, by ignorance of basic strategic reality on the part of Churchill. With the Italian Army in tatters it might have been possible for the whole of Libya to have been cleared had all the British forces been kept concentrated. As the Italians began to fall apart, Churchill directed a shift of resources to Greece in what the army commanders on the spot regarded as a hopeless effort: if the Germans attacked Greece no amount of British help could have saved the Greeks. Thus the British lost

out on both fronts, unable to deny the Germans in the Balkans, unable to clear the North African coast. While strategy must serve political ends (and it would have been difficult to let Greece to go the wall without some gesture of support) the strategic deployment of troops. must be in accordance with reality and what may be possible.

Nine days after Beda Fomm was fought two German battalions arrived in Tripoli. They were the leading elements of what was to become the Afrika Korps under Lieutenant General (later Field Marshal) Erwin Rommel. With the arrival of the Germans the war in North Africa was to last another twenty-seven months, though the issue was more or less resolved in October-November 1942. Rommel was undoubtedly a tactical genius and in conditions of fluid fighting more than a match for any British general pitted against him. But few campaigns bring home the importance of logistics, time and space, and of the inter-meshing of land, air and sea operations and their strategic effect than does the North African campaign. Every bullet, every item of clothing,food and supply, every litre of petrol (gasolene)

had to be brought to the theatre of operations since there were no sources of supply in the desert itself. The Axis forces in North Africa were supplied across the Mediterranean: the British either around the Cape or across the continent itself via the west coast, Chad, Sudan and Egypt. The amount of Axis supply was directly related to the scale of British naval activity from Malta but if the Germans held Libya (in addition to Crete) the supply of Malta could be made virtually prohibitive. But unless Malta was supplied there was little hope of breaking the German grip in Libya. In trying to clear the coastal area of the enemy both sides amply demonstrated the validity of the concept of 'the diminishing force of the offensive,' the weakening of an offensive effort as the toll of exhaustion and the drag of logistics began to make themselves felt. At the same time, while the attacker was moving away from his supplies on ever lengthening lines of communications, the defender was falling back on his support, growing in strength while the attacker weakened. So while there were considerable tactical successes for both sides there was no decisive strategic success in the theatre until 1943.

Tactically the war in the desert was dominated by the need for speed and surprise since there was no cover. In all his operations Rommel attempted to get around an open flank and into the British defensive system with his armour. Perhaps his most classic performance was at Gazala in May-June 1942, which ended with the capture of Tobruk. The battle had been extremely confused, with Rommel at one stage virtually out of supplies and trapped against the British minefields inside the British defensive zone. The British, however, had been unable to concentrate their armour and had fed it in piecemeal in the battles of May 28/29. The overall result was that they suffered a shattering defeat, while the Germans penetrated deeply into Egypt until halted outside a place called El Alamein. Rommel had begun Gazala with 560 German and Italian tanks; he reached Alamein with 55, and only 29 of the 88-mm guns that had repeatedly caught the British armour in the open at Gazala. At the end of a very long line of communications, and with a desperate shortage of petrol (gasolene), Rommel had to face a revitalized British Army drawing on supply dumps only sixty miles away. The British forces, moreover, were receiving new tanks and guns on a scale never experienced before: the fall of Tobruk had led the Americans to despatch 300 tanks and a hundred 105mm self-propelled guns immediately. To add to his problems, Rommel faced a continuous front at Alamein since there was no open flank. The British front rested on the sea in the north and the Qattara Depression in the south. An initial attempt to rush the position failed, as did a subsequent, more deliberate effort; then the battle died. The Germans were too weak to take the initiative but for political reasons could not retreat; the British were too weak and unready to take the initiative. The inescapable laws of supply and exhaustion imposed their will on the battlefield. It was not until October that the British moved. By then they had built up a 5:2 superiority in tanks, 2:1 in men and a definite edge in the air. The stage was set for a battle that was not characteristic of those fought in the desert during World War II, a battle of attrition, with the British attempting to force their way through the German positions in the north by clearing two corridors through the minefields in the hope of having enough battleworthy armour at the end to exploit the breach. They relied entirely on numbers, weight of firepower and sheer doggedness in order to wear down an inferior enemy. Ultimately they were successful in breaking into and through the Axis positions but were not able to encircle and annihilate the enemy, and the greater part of the German forces was able to escape. But the price of the British success was high – 13,500 dead with some 500 tanks and 100 guns out of action – but not high in comparison with the losses inflicted on the Axis. It is worth noting, however, that for twice the number of British dead at Alamein the Germans had conquered France.

The problems of supply and shortage of manpower in the face of an aggressive and numerically superior enemy were, by November 1942, causing the Germans acute embarrassment not only in North Africa but in Russia. At first the campaign in the east had gone well for the Germans, but never well enough since imprecision of objectives (the failure of strategic direction) and the problems of maintenance and supply imposed fateful delays on the German advance of 1941. The invasion itself, Operation Barbarossa, began on June 22, 1941 with a three-front assault (four if the Finns are included). The main weight of the attack was to the north of the Pripet Marshes with two separate and diverging objectives – Leningrad and the clearing of the Baltic coast on the one hand, Moscow on the other. The thrust on Moscow – for many of the planners the only worthwhile target since it was the seat of government, an armaments centre and at the hub of the

FINLAND

L. Onega

Helsinki

Gulf of Finland

L. Ladoga

Tallinn

Leningrad

Baltic Sea

Estonia

**Limit of Axis advance
(Dec. 1941)**

Novgorod

Pskov

Volga

Latvia

Riga

1

Gorky

Daugavpils

Dvina

Moscow

Memel

Lithuania

Niemen

Smolensk

**Limit of Axis advance
(Dec. 1941)**

E.
PRUSSIA

Kaunas

**Army Group
North**

Dniepr

Oka

Minsk

2

Belorussia

Bryansk

R   U   S   S   I   A

Warsaw

Orel

**Army Group
Centre**

Brest-Litovsk

Pripet

Pripet Marshes

Desna

POLAND

Kursk

Don

**Limit of Axis Advance
(Oct. 1942)**

**Front Line
Oct. 1941**

Lwow

Kharkov

3

U   k   r   a   i   n   e

**Army Group
South**

Dniepr

Stalingra

Donnets

HUNGRARY

Dniestr

Bug

Don

Rostov

Odessa

Sea of Azov

RUMANIA

Crimea

Bucharest

Sevastopol

Danube

**Limit of Axis advance
(Nov. 1942)**

Sofia

B   l   a   c   k   S   e   a

Caucasu

BULGARIA

200m

300km

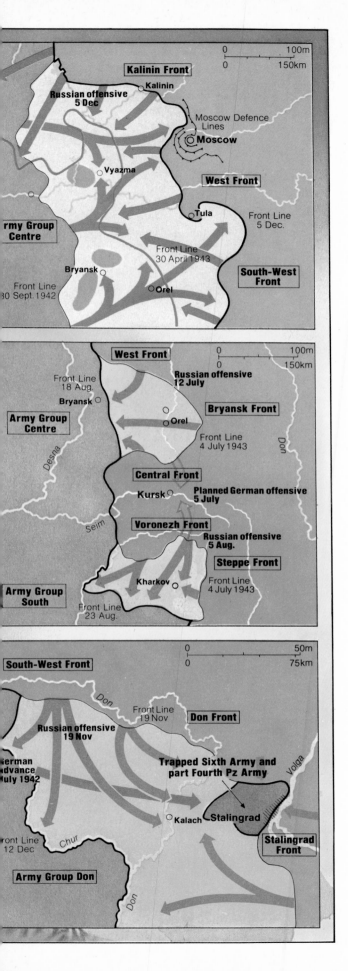

The German invasion of Soviet Russia reached the suburbs of Moscow and the banks of the Volga, but foundered in huge spoiling battles like the winter offensive at Moscow and the protracted battle of Stalingrad. The huge tank battle at Kursk finally guaranteed that Germany would lose the war. From 1943 onwards she fought a long withdrawal across Russia, Poland and the Balkans until Russian troops burst into Germany.

whole of the Soviet rail system – was made dependent on the outcome of the secondary battle, the clearing of the coast and control of Leningrad. To the south of the Pripet Marshes, German forces in and around Lublin were to attack towards Kiev with the object of trapping Soviet forces in the west and south Ukraine. The immediate tactical aim of the Germans was the entrapment of the Soviet Armies in front of the Dvina and Dneipr river line in order to prevent their retreat into the interior. Certainly Soviet deployment forward into these areas made them particularly vulnerable, but the notion of trying to catch them there begged a very important question: that before the rivers there were no cities of major importance that could act as centres of deployment for reserves being brought to the front. The German dilemma was therefore whether to rush the panzers forward on very thin axes of advance with their flanks wide open or very vulnerable, or to hold them back. If the panzers were held back they could assist the infantry (over 80 per cent of the Germany Army) in the reduction of the pockets of resistance that had been encircled by the panzers' initial thrust; but if they were held back, the panzers would not be able to move against the hinterland and would leave unthreatened for the moment the distant mobilization centres. If the panzers were moved forward then they faced the obvious problems of supply and maintenance on lengthening and difficult lines of communication, with enemy pockets still in their rear. Events were to show that the German infantry needed the armour to reduce pockets whose resistance seemed to be inversely related to their chances of success. But the real problem that developed in the summer of 1941 was twofold: exhaustion (particularly of machines in the dust and heat) and the intoxication of success. Exhaustion is obvious; the intoxicating belief that they had already won the war, led to the proliferation of effort on secondary targets at the expense of the main object. As the Soviet Armies scattered, the central thrust was weakened in order to help events along in the Ukraine, where the diverted help was not needed; the German success in the south drew them ever eastwards, far beyond initial objectives and supply capabilities. With all the delays during the summer caused by allocation of priorities and re-equipment, the final thrust on Moscow itself from the start line of Smolensk/ the river Desna began in late September 1941, the two armoured pincers on the flanks aiming for Vyazma and Bryansk in an effort to clear the way to the Soviet capital. The Germans took their initial objectives very quickly and the route to Moscow seemed wide open. The Soviets were on the horns of a dilemma. From Vyazma the Germans could advance on several axes – either directly upon Moscow or to the north or the south of the city. The Soviets had, moreover, very little left with which to fight: German intelligence estimated Soviet losses to date at about 2½ million men, 20,000 tanks and a similar number of guns. On the other hand, the Germans had their problems; re-supply was breaking down and their losses were heavy. By December, rail supply was only about one quarter of what was needed, and some divisions were little more than regiments. The autumn rains and mud slowed the advance, in some places stopped it altogether. The shortening days limited the hours of conflict and advance and severely curtailed the activities of the Luftwaffe. Moreover, the Soviets, favoured by the miles of forests before Moscow that slowed the rate of advance and limited the room for German manoeuvre and confident of the coming of a winter whose fury no European army had ever survived, had two priceless assets: a general of genius, Georgi Zhukov, and the last of the reserves, the twenty-five infantry divisions and nine tank brigades of the Far East, moved from that area when it became obvious that the Japanese did not intend to move against the USSR but to the south.

Zhukov's strategic objective was the retention of Moscow, the loss of which would have led to the isolation and almost certain collapse of both flanks. This had to be achieved by keeping what remained of his armies intact until the onset of winter; resistance had to be effective to keep the Germans at bay, but mobile enough to keep out of range of the encircling German armoured pincers. To fight this battle Zhukov had very few good troops, and those that he did have, he wished to hold back until the whole of the German effort was spent. So he used his worker battalions and *ad hoc* army units to meet the initial attack and his one and only tank brigade against Guderian's IInd Panzer Army, advancing from Orel to slow this assault while thinning the other fronts in order to build up armour reserves on the flanks while holding in the centre. The final German thrust on Moscow broke through to Dmitrov and Ryazan, but the ferocity of Soviet resistance, the extreme cold and German exhaustion enabled the flanks to hold, while on December 6 the Siberians, for the most part uncommitted up until this stage, went over to the offensive in the centre. In tem-

peratures which fell to −63°C Soviet tactics, massed armoured and infantry attacks along predictable axes of advance, mauled the Germans badly. Moscow was saved by this counter-attack and the Germans never again tried the direct approach on the capital. With Leningrad besieged, and the front in that area stabilized after the Soviet failure to relieve the city, attention switched to the south.

One of the little known facts to emerge from World War II is that the Germans secured more industrial and agricultural produce from the Soviet Union between 1939 and 1941 than they did from their period of occupation of parts of the USSR between 1941 and 1944. For Hitler in 1942 – having added the USA to his list of enemies – strategy dictated that Germany had to force a decision in 1942 and that he had to secure the Ukraine, the Donbas and the oil of the Caucasus. Without the natural resources of these areas Germany could not hope to win the war; with the defeat of the Soviet Union the task facing the Allies would have been virtually impossible. Germany was forced to attack in the south in 1942.

For the Germans the 1942 campaign started well. Although they had taken reverses in the winter, including the loss of Rostov, the Soviet spring offensive around Kharkov resulted in the destruction of the Soviet forces committed to the attack and the leaving of the eastern Ukraine wide open to a German advance. At Kharkov, the Soviets needed close co-ordination between their forces to avoid defeat because for this attack they had no margin of superiority over the Germans. They attempted to batter their way through the German positions north of Kharkov and were able to tear a gap some seventy miles wide in the German front, but their inexperience in moving forward across razed countryside away from supply dumps, led to confusion. As German resistance stiffened on the flanks of the breach and the Soviets pushed deeper into the German positions, their chances of escaping from the inevitable counter-attack diminished. Because of the stupidity of Stalin the offensive was maintained long after any hope for success had passed and the prospects for annihilation had become almost certain. At the end of May the Germans sealed the breach and encircled the Soviets, the latter losing 200,000 prisoners and 1000 tanks. In its own way the battle around Kharkov was one of the most effective battles of riposte fought in the war.

The subsequent German offensive that sought to

exploit this situation started well, quickly securing a firm flank in the capture of Voronezh. The thrust of the advance, however, was both southwards towards Armavir, Maikop, Grozny and Baku (1st Panzer Army) and eastwards (4th Panzer and 6th Armies) towards the Volga, the initial aim being to secure the flank for the southwards move but with the long-term objective of moving up the Volga towards Kazan, thus outflanking Moscow from the east. Via a string of impressive victories, this offensive led the Germans to utter defeat at Stalingrad. That city was merely the stop point for the attack, the location on the Volga on which the flank should be pinned. But the Germans failed to take the city in its first rush (August 19) and both sides began to feed in their reserves. But whereas the Soviets fed in reserves on the basis of the minimum necessary, the Germans began to feed men in on the basis of the maximum possible in a desperate effort to break Soviet will. Thus, while the Soviets were able to build up most of their reserves on the flanks for the counterattack, the Germans exposed themselves to a situation whereby their panzers and elite infantry were ground down in street fighting (where their supreme attributes of mobility and firepower were discounted), stationary at the very tip of a stalled advance. The German flanks, moreover, were in the air. They were held by the inadequately equipped Rumanian and Italian armies while the Soviets held many bridgeheads in the bend of the Don. Totally absorbed by the battle for

Stalingrad the Germans ignored these bridgeheads: the Soviets did not and it was from them that the Soviets launched their strikes against the Rumanians on November 19. For the offensives on either side of Stalingrad, the Soviets deployed a million men, over 13,000 guns and 900 tanks formed into 66 rifle divisions, 18 mechanized brigades, 5 tank corps and 14 brigades, 3 cavalry corps and 127 artillery regiments. Given the shortage of artillery the opening barrage had to last as long as eighty minutes and the shortage of ground troops generally meant that the attack lacked depth, with the armour held back for the exploitation of a breach made primarily by infantry. On the northern flank, however, the tanks had to pass through the infantry in order to make the breach themselves. But the breaches were made and despite the problems of navigation over the featureless Steppes, and the chaos both on and off the pincers closed at Kalach. The entombed Germans in Stalingrad numbered some 250,000 men, 100 tanks and 2000 guns, a force roughly three times as strong as the Soviets had anticipated. It was not until February 2, 1943 that incessant Soviet pressure, the bitterness of the weather and starvation finally brought about the end of desperate resistance. Until that time the German position in Stalingrad tied down a considerable part of the Soviet forces in the south, thus making it more difficult for them to pursue German forces to the west in the central Ukraine.

In operations involving relatively short distances in

Left: Germans on the defensive in Russia. Pioneers dig in frozen snow in the winter of 1943/44 to lay Teller anti-tank mines. Right:
Soviet sailors man a multi-barrelled Maxim machine-gun on an anti-aircraft mount. Though the Soviet anti-aircraft defences were almost non-existent at the beginning of the Battle of Stalingrad they improved steadily until the beleagured German 6th Army was denied most of its airborne supplies by a ring of heavy and medium anti-aircraft guns.

the offensive and with only severely weakened opposition in the way, the Red Army at Stalingrad showed that it could penetrate a front and then encircle and annihilate an enemy. But a more ambitious offensive in the Kharkov direction in February/March 1943 produced the same result as the offensive of May 1942, the Germans demonstrating their strategic and tactical superiority over the Soviets at this stage of the war. As the Soviets pushed to the south west in the face of light resistance, the Germans thinned their front and gave ground, building up fresh panzer forces on the flanks ready for the counter-attack. The Germans were confident once again that the further the Soviets advanced the greater the ultimate German victory, but German infantry scarcity meant that when the trap was sprung much of the Soviet force was able to evade the pincers and escape. The Soviet offensive, however, which had threatened to destroy the whole of the German position in the central and eastern Ukraine, was brought to nothing and the front stabilized roughly along the line from which the Germans had started in May 1942.

There were, however, two vital differences from the situation in May 1942. Firstly, crises were brewing for the Germans in the Mediterranean with the surrender of Axis forces in Tunisia, while the power of the USA was being increasingly felt in the European war; and secondly, the Red Army was now such a threat that it had to be brought to battle and defeated. The configuration of the front determined where the Germans should make their effort. From the Baltic to Orel the front was solid, almost World War I style with trenches, permanent emplacements, and minefields. To the south lay the Kursk salient that overhung the German positions in the Ukraine. Here the Germans hoped to bring to battle the bulk of Soviet armour and to defeat it. Here, too, the Soviets were prepared to give battle in the calculation that in such an encounter the Germans would have to come to them. The Soviets trusted that their tenacity in defence plus weight of shot would prove decisive. To this end, in the defence of the salient the Soviets ultimately deployed about 1,337,000 troops, 20,220 artillery pieces and 3306 tanks plus an extra tank army in reserve. The defence system was some 110 miles deep across the neck of the salient and consisted largely of groups of five 76.2mm AT guns sited in batteries, mutually supporting, and backed by mortars, engineers and infantry. Extensive minefields were laid – on average about 5000 mines to the mile – in order to channel the German thrusts onto the batteries where weight of broadside rather than individual shots would hopefully deal with the tanks. In immediate support were tanks, hull down, with medium artillery, and behind these more tanks either to help in the defence or, more hopefully, held for the counter-attack once the Germans were halted and exhausted. Tactically the Germans relied more or less on the *blitzkrieg* technique with the new Tiger tanks in the van, the lighter tanks on the flanks and in the rear. But in the north they attempted to punch a series of separate holes through the Soviet defences in order to feed tanks through the breach, just as the British had done at Alamein, but in this case without the assured superiority of numbers and equipment that Montgomery had enjoyed.

The battle was predictable (at least in retrospect) in that as in World War I the attackers broke into but not through the defences, and the counter-attack eliminated all the attackers' gains. German losses in men and tanks – possibly as high as 1200 tanks – were so high that the Soviets were able to push on for the rest of the summer, beyond the Dneipr, liberating Kiev and Poltava in the process. In this, as in all subsequent Soviet offensives, thrusts were noted for their strategic and organizational flexibility if not their

tactical finesse. Their tactics in the offensive were characterized by heavy artillery concentration and a broad frontage of attack with either a mixed infantry or tank assault in double echelon, pressing hard on an initial reconnaissance. (Various attempts were made to launch three- or four-echelon attacks to give depth but these were abandoned because, inevitably, they reduced to unacceptably low levels the weight of firepower in the assault.) The Soviets aimed to make one or two breaches and, thinning the front but still holding the enemy along it, transfer the overwhelming part of the attacking force into the breach(es) for exploitation. Soviet tactical practice in the initial tank assault was interesting for reasons that even now may still be applicable. In the early days of the war tank divisions were quite literally used until they took 100 per cent casualties. Later they were more carefully used, in that exhausted divisions were pulled out when roughly at brigade strength and then used as shock divisions, having been strengthened by some infantry and tank reinforcements and with a full division's allocation of artillery. These divisions operated on very narrow frontages: in one case only 700m (700 yards) wide. In the event of a breakthrough being achieved, the division then lost its artillery support. Moreover,

committing tanks to an initial assault was invariably very costly, yet towards the end of the war the Soviets frequently resorted to massed tank attacks at the start of operations, possibly because they were prepared to suffer high losses that might be incurred anyway and probably also because their overwhelming superiority of numbers allowed them to be somewhat prodigal. These attacks had little infantry support but many repair and maintenance parties. Only about one in three tanks knocked out were unfit for repair and the Soviets worked on a system of the momentum (and overall strength) of an attack being maintained by the repair and relief crews. This did lead to the situation whereby the Soviets could lose two to three times as many tanks as they had at the start and still have some left at the end of the battle.

German defensive tactics in the face of mounting Soviet power was to try to make the initial assault hit air by withdrawal immediately before the attack. This needed good field intelligence, which was generally available. Armour was held back to deal with breakthroughs with the main killing zones covered by light, medium and heavy anti-tank weapons. Though very effective such tactics could never do more than delay or exact a heavy toll on the attacker; they could never

Patton in a new war meets Montgomery also fighting – the two generals were rivals for the honours of clearing France and breaking into Germany. Below: American troops in street fighting in Tangemunde. A BAR gunner takes aim round a corner to cover his comrade as he moves up the street.

79th Armoured Division. Amphibious tanks led the assault to the water's edge from where they engaged enemy strong points; they were followed by flail tanks to beat a way through the minefields and then by tanks with bridging equipment or fascines to climb sea walls and cross anti-tank ditches. Flame-throwing tanks were used to reduce points of resistance, and in order to prevent tanks and wheeled vehicles being stranded in soft sand a modified Churchill tank chassis laid a 9′ 11″ wide canvas cover in front of itself as a road.

The fighting on the beaches was generally successful in all cases with unexceptional losses but, except for the almost unopposed American landings in southern France, the Allies found great difficulty in moving off the beaches into open country. In Sicily, at Anzio and Normandy the Allies found themselves sealed in by very effective German resistance. To break out they, particularly the British, had to fight battles of attrition – heavily relying on naval gunfire and tactical air power – to 'write-down' German armour that was qualitatively far superior to their own. At Normandy, Montgomery used narrow frontal attacks, armour heavy, to grip the German armour in Operations Epsom and Goodwood, while the Americans, faced by less powerful forces, used their heavy strategic bombers to blast a path through the German defences in Operation Cobra.

Strategically the Allied advance from Normandy across France to the German border was dogged by problems of logistics and personality. The broad front approach favoured by Eisenhower had the advantage of keeping the pressure on the Germans across the whole of the front and keeping them off-balance; the narrow front approach – favoured by Montgomery as long as it was not his forces that were held back – had the advantage of possibly delivering a knock-out blow by concentrating a maximum effort to take advantage of Germany's parlous state. The weakness of this argument was that in order to concentrate for a single attack all the other fronts would have to be closed down, though this was going to be inevitable at some stage or another given the problem of supply. In the end a narrow front attack was adopted in Operation Market Garden, the crossing of the Rhine by a land advance via bridges captured and held by airborne troops. The weakness of this particular operation was the predictability of the axes of advance once the parachute force had landed, a minimal use of the great assets of numbers and mobility since the land operation

give the Germans any hope of regaining the strategic initiative.

Anglo-American strategy in the European context was determined not by what they wanted to do but by two things – the outcome of the war at sea (fundamentally resolved in summer 1943) and the availability of troops, shipping and landing craft, none of which were plentiful before 1943. The lack of landing ships plus the fact that North Africa was already a major theatre of war led the first Anglo-American efforts to be in the Mediterranean against Sicily and Italy. This was portrayed as attempting to penetrate the 'soft underbelly' of Europe and was subsequently justified in political terms – concern over the Balkans, influence on Turkey, etc. In reality there was no option. Though a cross-Channel assault would have been desirable, such an action was impossible before 1944.

Caution and prudence dominated Anglo-American tactics: great care was taken to minimize losses and to avoid the likelihood of defeat. The latter was particularly in evidence during seaborne landings when defeat on the beaches could result not simply in the defeat of that particular invasion but the ruining of future prospects, with incalculable results. Thus Patton's more imaginative plan for invading Sicily by landings around both Palermo and Syracuse was set aside in favour of Montgomery's more cautious one to concentrate all forces around Cape Passero – within the range of air cover, with undivided fire support from the sea and with the land forces enjoying a greater concentration of firepower than they would have had had they been split. At Normandy the same process was repeated with the landing beaches concentrated along a narrow front and (with one exception) within two river lines, the bridges over which were the targets of airborne assault. Much ingenuity went into solving the tactical problems of forcing an advance across open beaches into open country, the British particularly being well supplied with specialist tanks from the

Above: platoons have deployed off a road and a despatch rider has arrived with others.

Below: the platoon is dug in and while one man stands down his comrade remains on guard.

Nagasaki in October 1945. The Atomic bombs ushered in a new era in warfare in which many people believed that old lessons and experience were valueless. However, smaller, localized wars since 1945 have showed that terrain and men remain the same and war presents similar challenges.

was by definition a long narrow penetration with the firepower of the assault limited to its lead elements and, finally, poor intelligence and planning. The attack also suffered from the insoluble problem that the armour was forced to use roads raised above the level of the surrounding countryside, thus leaving the tanks silhouetted and vulnerable to German anti-tank guns. The operation failed and it can be argued that the effort spent in Market Garden could have been far more profitably employed in clearing the Germans from their positions on the banks of the Wester Schelde, thereby opening the sea route into the port of Antwerp that had been captured intact. Had this happened the Allied offensive into Germany might well have taken place far earlier.

Supply in this case was vital, as it was in the Pacific theatre. The war here was primarily a sea and land war to which land warfare, though intense on occasions and vitally important, was subordinate. The story of the Pacific war illustrates as few campaigns could, the immense flexibility of sea power and results that can be achieved by the combination of military and sea power. Japan was beaten to her knees even before Hiroshima in a war decided in the Pacific to which events in Burma, China and Manchuria were totally subordinate. Yet the blasting of Hiroshima and Nagasaki marked not an end but a new beginning. The surrender of Germany, Italy and Japan, and the devastation of Europe and vast areas of the Far East were witness to the fact that the old order had passed beyond recall. Already divisions among the Allies were obvious and the world was being divided ideologically between the superpowers, both of whom sought allegiance and support from the defeated and the neutral. In the areas they occupied the superpowers were to tolerate only mirror images of their own societies. The great colonial empires were in turmoil, particularly in Asia, but even in areas that had not been directly affected by war, change was in the air as nationalist aspirations began to surface. With these changes went the development of new and more powerful weapons of destruction that were to change the face of warfare itself.

War in The Third World

Mao Tse-tung in the early days of his guerrilla war.
He is the father of all post-war insurgencies.

Mao delivers a speech at Kangta, the Chinese people's anti-Japanese Military and Political College. His writings and propaganda are now widely translated and though heavy reading give an insight into the planning, patience and ruthless energy that motivated the Chinese Communist revolution. Other revolutionaries have used his name and some of his ideas in their own battles.

The techniques and tactics of guerrilla warfare are probably the oldest forms of warfare known to man, but the uses to which these forms have been put, and the context in which they have operated during the last thirty years, do bestow upon guerrilla warfare elements of novelty. In the past, guerrilla warfare was employed as one of the means by which nations fought one another (the Spanish and Russians against Napoleon; the French in 1871 against the Germans) but since 1945 it has become a method used to conduct and resolve internal political disputes. Since 1945 there has been an increasing employment of revolutionary guerrilla warfare – the application of guerrilla warfare method to revolutionary objectives, particularly in the context of national liberation in colonies. Given the Soviet view of 'peaceful co-existence,' (the destruction of Western capitalist society by any method short of war), wars of national liberation will remain despite the absence of colonial regimes, the target being governments of countries that oppose communism.

The concepts of revolutionary guerrilla warfare are a synthesis of the writings of various political and military writers and of the practical experience, writings and example of various individuals, most notably the leader of the largest such campaign ever fought, Mao Tsetung. Mao drew from his hard-learned experiences in China, the writings of such military analysts as Sun Tze, Clausewitz, T. E. Lawrence, and his interpretation of Marxist-Leninism, a concept of warfare that was simple and straightforward, explaining it to and impressing it upon his colleagues. In effect, he provided a do-it-yourself guide that through a dogged and unwavering dedication to his model, he finally made work in 1949. By success he invited emulation and just as the Russian pattern of revolution became the established method of revolution after its 1917 success, so the Maoist pattern became the established norm after 1949.

Mao Tse-tung developed a strategy based on guerrilla warfare that allowed an under-industrialized and primitive society, lacking modern arms and equipment, to adopt a militant political philosophy based on armed struggle. From this fundamental premise, Mao developed a military doctrine that enabled a backward society such as China to adopt a political posture and form a resistance even when confronted with the militarily superior forces of a highly industrialized state – hence its continued relevance. Naturally within this context Mao measured

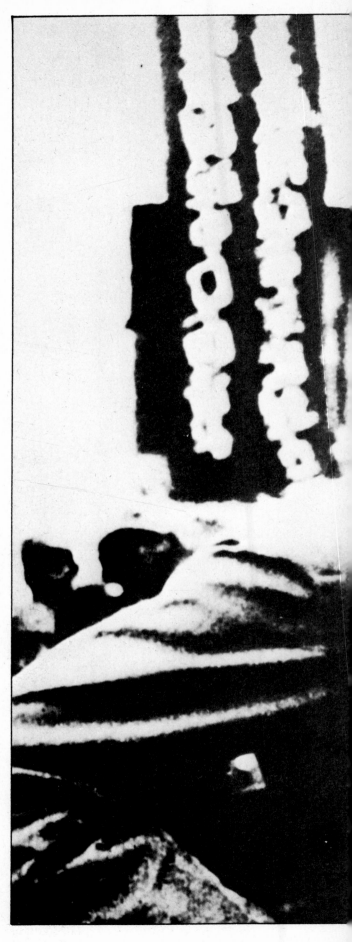

The weapons and men at Dien Bien Phu. The French and Colonial forces were well equipped with American 105-mm guns and light tanks, but though their paratroops (below) had modern weapons they were ill prepared for the Viet Minh artillery. The Viet Minh soldier (below right) was highly motivated, tough and driven by efficient political officers who realized that though they might suffer heavy casualties these were more than acceptable if they could achieve victory in time for the Geneva peace talks.

military potential by standards very different from Western, even Soviet, norms. In the West military effectiveness is chiefly equated with weapons systems, logistics and trained manpower; Mao, faced by an absence of these three commodities, claimed that revolutionary military effectiveness had to be measured in political terms. Accepting war as a form of politics and that revolutionary warfare was nothing if not political, Mao argued that military factors must always be subordinate to ideological phenomena. Thus he relegated purely military considerations to the background, or, more accurately, made them dependent upon political factors. A careful reading of *Protracted Warfare* and *Strategy in the Guerrilla War Against the Japanese Invaders* reveals that to Mao the decisive factors in war are will (the political morale of society), time (which will exhaust the superior resources of the sophisticated society) and space (essential for the exploitation of time and will).

Thus to summarize Mao's writings, the revolutionary's only chance of defeating a superior enemy lies in his ability to raise the population. Once this is achieved, space and manpower provide time. Time was the equalizing factor between the sides since (writing of Japan) '. . . in spite of . . . industrial progress . . . her manpower, her raw materials and her financial resources are all inadequate and insufficient to maintain her in protracted war or to meet the situation presented by a war prosecuted over a vast area.' Mao appreciated the need for an industrialized society to force the issue quickly: his intention in guerrilla warfare was to avoid a decision, ensuring an enemy's tactical success could not be translated into strategic victory. He thereby prolonged war to a point where it became politically

and economically unacceptable to the enemy. This is the basis of communist faith in ultimate victory in war, irrespective of the duration of the struggle.

Mao saw his strategy as a series of three merging phases, the first of which was the mobilization and organization of the people in order to maintain the eventual military effort. In this first phase the aim was to establish safe bases, free from outside interference, in which the population could be brought under control and during which military preparations could be commenced. In this phase fighting was subordinate to indoctrination, control and organization. The building up of local home guard units, intelligence networks and the training of regular units were the priority. Emphasis was placed on political objectives that would be sympathetically received by the population and upon the correct treatment of the population by the army. Mao had seen a ruthless policy of coercion by the communists backfire disastrously in the twenties while in the thirties the effect of the casual and deliberate barbarity of the Japanese was obvious to anyone with eyes. By sound and fair administration, reforms, mildness of taxation, popular support could be obtained; by use of mass organizations and popular slogans, society could be orchestrated. Thus regimented, society and the revolutionary soldier were linked inescapably together: what was in reality a piecemeal process of national reconstruction allowed the creation of the water (friendly civilian attitudes) in which the fish (the revolutionary soldier) could operate. During the second phase, the military preparations were put in hand in the form of guerrilla action in the attempt to disperse, immobilize and break down the resolve of the enemy, while at the same time building

up experience, improving organization and securing arms. This in itself was a self-generating process in that it brought under control new areas and more people for political mobilization. In northern China between 1937 and 1945 communist forces expanded from a single base area to control fourteen major zones inside Japanese-held territory. The final phase of protracted war was conventional or positional warfare. Guerrilla warfare in itself could not achieve victory but could only pave the way for it. Victory had to be secured by regular formations exploiting the favourable conditions achieved by the first two phases, in the last phase, the roused countryside moving in to engulf the towns. From this basic framework two subsequent points emerge. Firstly, the flexibility of the model in that the whole process was reversible on meeting a check and the cycle then recommenced. Secondly, the final phase could be curtailed by negotiations but only for the purpose of securing a surrender: in other phases they could be used to secure a respite. Negotiations were a means to an end: there was no element of good faith in such undertakings.

Mao's concepts worked well enough in China though it must be noted that his success owed as much to the failings, incompetence and divisions of the opposition as to the strength and potency of communist insurgency. In other areas, they did not do so well, as in Malaya where a combination of governmental resolution, severity, enlightened administration and the provision of security combined to stem the communists. In Malaya, a lack of space in which to manoeuvre in order to avoid defeat while not losing touch with (and some degree of control over) the population was a grave handicap for the insurgents. In order to survive as government counter-measures began to exact their

toll, the communists had to move away from the battle area – the Chinese shantytowns that lined the jungle fringe – and move into the *ulu*. Counter-insurgent tactics in this phase of the struggle were the basic ambush and intense, long patrolling: the aim was to control the jungle around settled areas to a depth of five hours marching time. In time this proved very successful as the jungle craft of the security forces improved and outstripped that of the insurgents. Nevertheless it was the accumulation of pressure that led to the communists breaking off the struggle in the settled areas, and here the British relied on a variety of measures that were retained after independence in 1957. Foremost among them was the resettlement and concentration of the population under close and increasingly effective police surveillance. Material inducements to the population (tactically raising the level of the campaign from a competition in coercion to one of government in which the communists, given their resources, could not compete), the liberalization of the naturalization laws and a tightening denial programme of all types of supply, particularly food, were the chief measures by which the government secured firstly control and then the support of the population. Added to these, was a streamlining and extremely close co-ordination of administration, police and military efforts of which the police were arguably the most important. Gradually recovering from a very shaky start and growing in effectiveness with an influx of new weapons, communications and, above all, manpower (particularly Chinese) it was the police, operating within the security gradually built up by the army around the villages, who identified and eliminated the communists within the battle zone. This was achieved by the systematic clearing of the country area by area, concentrating on the

weakest communist areas first before moving on the more badly affected areas later.

Nevertheless insurgent failure in Malaya – and in such places as the Philippines – could be attributed to exceptional local factors such as Malaya's isolation, the fact that the insurgency was almost exclusively based on one racial group, the missed opportunities of 1945–49 that gave the government both warning and time in which to act effectively to deny the communists victory. The 1948–60 failure can also be explained away as being only the first round in a struggle which is still going on, the final outcome of which is by no means clear. In any event the Maoist concepts were put into practice in various places, most notably in nearby Indo-China where Truong Van Chinh, better known as Ho Chi Minh, closely followed Mao's ideas and whose book *The Resistance Will Win* became the revolutionary gospel of the Viet Minh in the war against the French, 1946–54. Certain modifications were provided after 1950 by the appearance of *The War of Liberation and the People's Army* by Ho Chi Minh's chief lieutenant, V. N. Giap.

Giap accepted virtually all of Mao's ideas but modified the final stage in which he considered four conditions were necessary before a final offensive could be undertaken. He believed that insurgent forces had to achieve a marked psychological ascendancy over the enemy and to have confidence in their ability to win in conditions of conventional fighting while there was a declining offensive spirit in the enemy camp. Further, possibly because he was operating in a colony, Giap believed that an essential requirement had to be a favourable international situation or climate of opinion. Both against the French and the Americans, the communists had more than one eye on the psychological

impact of military actions and, indeed, both campaigns were characterized by the insidious confidence-sapping psychological offensive against the enemy homeland and population. In both instances, the wavering of determination in the effort of the counter-insurgents took place before defeat in the field occurred. Moreoever, to the practice of revolutionary guerrilla warfare, Giap contributed the deliberate and systematic use of terrorism against the population, not simply to coerce the people and totally commit the perpetrators but to undermine the society against which he was pitted. Using terrorism in the late fifties and early sixties, the Hanoi-controlled Viet Cong as a matter of policy exterminated the village leaders and government officials of South Vietnam in order to destroy the stability of the society they sought to undermine. The consequence of such actions was that in many areas of South Vietnam, government except by the Viet Cong ceased to exist and, unlike the British in Malaya who had to maintain and then expand a threatened but existing political infrastructure, the South Vietnamese and Americans actually had to try to create one in the midst of a losing war and in conditions of utter loss of confidence on the part of the population in Saigon's authority. The idea of using terrorism was not new, of course, but Giap raised it to a level of intensity hitherto unknown.

The notion of using selective terrorism to undermine society was taken up in the late sixties by a Brazilian, Carlos Marighela. His ideas were to become increasingly important (and relevant) after the failure of numerous rural insurgency attempts throughout Latin America in the aftermath of Castro's successful campaign in Cuba (1956–59). In part the mainland failures resulted directly from Cuba in two respects. Firstly, Castro's success and subsequent drift into the communist camp alerted Latin American governments to the danger of insurgency: Cuba sacrificed by her success the priceless advantage of surprise. Moreover, Castro's links with Moscow squeezed the middle ground – the area of genuine doubt, uncertainty, confusion and tolerance essential for democracy as much as for its enemies – by forcing a choice between two monoliths, communism and the *status quo*. Such a choice crushed much potential support. Secondly, certain lessons were drawn from Cuba, most notably by Castro and Guevara, that became revolutionary dogma in Latin America in the sixties. These lessons were three in number. Firstly, that the security forces were not invincible and could be

beaten; secondly, that the countryside was the natural area of operations for the revolutionaries; thirdly, and most contentiously, Guevara argued that military action could produce the revolutionary situation necessary for insurgent success. This was in direct contradiction to Lenin's concepts of preparation while waiting for the profound crisis in society of which the communists hoped to take advantage. It was also a total rejection of Mao's emphasis on a long period of indoctrination of the population as the basis of military operations. Guevara argued that a small, mobile, hard-hitting nucleus of professional revolutionaries (called the *foco*) could, by military action, provoke the crisis and hence the momentum for success by tactical victories in the field – a bandwagon effect whereby success fed upon success, the credibility of the government being eroded by failure while insurgent victories brought an influx of recruits, supply and political sympathy.

Guevara's incompetent and disastrous Bolivian campaign in 1967 was sufficient comment on the validity of his ideas. The countryside, particularly in the Andean states, was simply not ripe for revolutionary insurgency. In no Latin American country in the sixties did rural insurgency survive to pose a major threat and only in five instances did campaigns even get beyond the preliminary stages. American training, personnel and equipment, reform programmes, the problems of movement, and poor fieldcraft, of the insurgents, the apathy of rural populations and the effectiveness of the security forces conspired to crush the revolutionary movements. But as the survivors of these attempts drifted back to the towns there dawned the slow realization of the revolutionary potential of the towns themselves, hitherto overlooked and in the case of Guevara, decried. In the sixties Latin America became more than 50 per cent urban for the first time. This in itself meant that rural insurgency was less relevant than it had been. In these rising and sprawling cities the pool of under- and unemployed, the young, the squatter population in the shanty towns beckoned as an immense reservoir of potential disaffection. The towns themselves were concentrations of power – and vulnerable targets – with easy access to the population

via the media. And the towns afforded cover, security and easy routes to and from targets. These were the points realized by the Tupamaros guerrillas in Uruguay and by Marighela. It was from the practical example of the former and the writings of the latter (*Handbook of Urban Guerrilla Warfare*) that there emerged the concept of urban-based insurgency which led to a global upsurge in this form of conflict in the early seventies.

Marighela concurred in Guevara's belief in the *foco* concept but differed in his approach. He believed that a revolutionary elite could precipitate revolution through armed struggle but he believed in an urban *foco* as the means of achieving this. The aim of urban revolutionary warfare was twofold. Firstly to draw the security forces into the towns and thereby weaken their grip on the countryside, thus allowing the insurgents to establish themselves in rural areas. Marighela believed that rural and urban insurgency had to complement each other, otherwise they would be defeated singly. Together they would unbalance the security forces and prevent their concentration, thus allowing the insurgency groups

The Vietnam war: Men of an American airborne division on patrol through secondary jungle. Behind the point man the patrol commander has positioned his grenade-launcher ready to engage the enemy should the patrol trigger an ambush. Contacts with the Viet Cong were often accidental and led to small, but steadily mounting casualties throughout the war.

room to manoeuvre. Secondly, urban guerrilla warfare tried to demoralize society by forcing the security forces into repression, thus polarizing society by revealing the repressive but impotent nature of the state to a disenchanted population. By a combination of criminal technique and astute manipulation of the media and of popular grievances, urban guerrilla warfare hoped to create a revolutionary groundswell by alienating people from authority. In short, urban guerrilla warfare was a sort of nationwide protection racket that tried to humiliate authority and lead to such a crisis of confidence that the population would turn to the insurgents for protection and as the only means of ending the struggle.

The darling of the academic revolutionary, Che Guevara, took the foci theory of revolutionary war to Bolivia and failed. The theory as expounded by Regis Debray required the revolutionary to plant himself in a country and win the people over by armed propaganda – it worked in Cuba, but failed in Bolivia where Guevara was killed. Inset: Fidel Castro the leader of the Cuban revolutionaries with the hunting rifle that was his personal weapon.

Marighela was killed in a clash with the Brazilian police in November 1969 but, unlike Guevara, this could not be considered as a comment on his ideas. But there were obvious weaknesses in the concept. Most notable was the fact that a government need not necessarily be forced into repression prior to an insurgent action of a kind that could alienate the population from the insurgents – a backlash in reverse. This in fact has happened in Turkey, in West Germany and, even before Marighela formulated his ideas, in Venezuela in the early sixties. Moreover, if there was a backlash against the insurgents it could result in a mild and tolerant government that hesitated to use repression being replaced by one that had no such scruples. In Uruguay the Tupamaros themselves were destroyed by exactly this process. A further difficulty, besides the obvious problem of liaison between rural and urban insurgent groups, was the expansion from small four- or five-strong groups whose survival depended on their security and elusiveness, into large scale organizations capable of taking the initiative and securing victory in the event of a weakening of authority. The strength of Marighela's concept was that it provided a do-it-yourself guide to aspiring guerrillas on the mechanics of urban insurgency. The *Handbook* outlined techniques, not political claims and strategy. This ensured imitation, particularly given the ease of communication of both people and ideas. The basic ideas of urban guerrilla warfare applied in Northern Ireland have tied down a considerable part of the British Army for a period longer than the duration of World War II.

The tactics used in Northern Ireland have been essentially those outlined by Marighela: raids and assaults (particularly on commercial, police and military establishments and on the methods of communication of the security forces), occupation of targets such as radio stations and factories (for propaganda effect), the basic ambush, the formation of street disturbances (often to draw the security forces into a killing zone), murder (euphemistically termed execution), kidnapping, sabotage and general, indiscriminate terrorism. While individual actions may vary in aim and be mounted for specific purposes – such as the liberating of hospitalized or imprisoned colleagues, securing weapons, eliminating police agents, etc. – the whole emphasis of action is placed on its psychological impact and value. Every action has to be geared to its morale value, a place on the evening television news, the next morning's newspaper headlines. Every action must

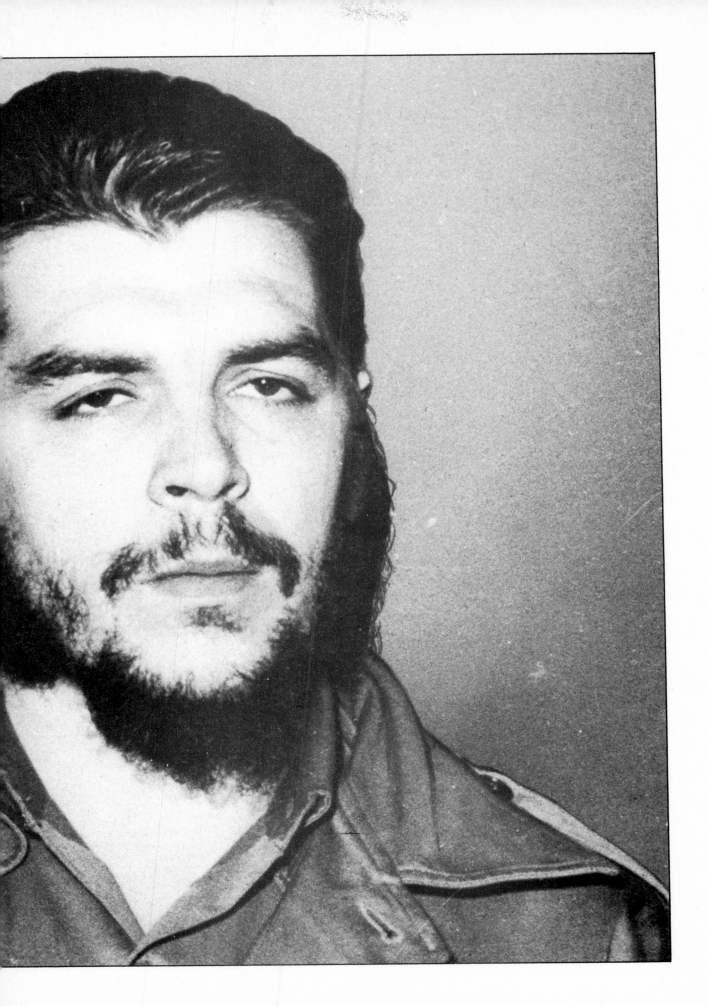

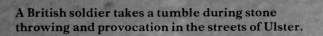

**A British soldier takes a tumble during stone
throwing and provocation in the streets of Ulster.**

be seen in this context. Two good examples of the way in which urban insurgents may attempt to seize the psychological advantage over the security forces can be indicated by the activities of the IRA. Prior to the meetings in September 1971 of the British, Irish and Northern Irish prime ministers, IRA bombings and shootings were stepped up to unprecedented intensity – diminishing the value of the talks themselves and forcing the meeting to react to events, rather than debate actions that could impose upon events. Similarly the bombings in central London on March 8, 1973 were deliberately designed to distract attention (particularly international attention) from the fact that that day Ulster voted by 591,820 votes to 6463 to stay in the United Kingdom. In both cases the presentation of photogenic violence tended to offset the political initiative of the governments concerned. This is not to argue that the physical damage that may be achieved in such actions is not without great importance in its own right; obviously it is. It is interesting to note that the original IRA campaign of 1919 opened with attacks on 119 Income Tax offices, actions bound to be popular with people but also striking directly at the heart of state power which lies in its ability to tax. Three hundred and fifteen abandoned police barracks were also attacked, seemingly a somewhat quixotic gesture until it is realized that any counter-offensive by the army and police in 1919 or 1920 could only have been based on their re-occupation of deserted stations. In the present campaign in Northern Ireland, a huge amount of damage has been caused, in part resulting from the calculation that the cost of the campaign can be made too high for the British.

Such have been some of the tactics used by urban terrorists. The primary objective has been to secure control over the population and to divide society against itself. It may be that the greatest weakness of urban guerrilla warfare is that it cannot polarize a society unless it is already divided. But it may also be that the second objective, the weakening of resolve on the part of authority, may also be beyond the reach of the insurgents since such operations will in future be bound to be undertaken in metropolitan homelands, not in far distant colonies or dependencies from which one can retreat.

The fact that they were fighting on what they considered to be home soil and that there was no place to which to withdraw in part may explain the vehemence of the French reaction to events in Algeria, 1954–62. France committed 500,000 men to the Algerian war and in military terms won the conflict. France isolated Algeria from external sources of succour by the creation of massive barriers along her frontiers and by intensive patrolling of the coasts. She resettled the population and garrisoned the country in strength, the size of garrisons being determined by the size and importance of the location. In the countryside the French used aggressive light units in scouting operations characterized by an unprecedented use of helicopters. At one stage, 600 helicopters were deployed and they quickly showed their advantage over other aircraft in being able either to airdrop or land forces in a closely compact group with none of the problems of re-organization after a jump. These tactics were employed in order to gain contact with enemy formations and to harrass them relentlessly to destruction. This task was mainly left to the elite formations in the French Army, such as the Legion, Paras, Marines and Chasseurs. Though extremely costly in money and prodigal in manpower, such tactics worked: by 1961 the military side of the insurgency was spent. But in making this effort the French dissipated the political advantage which was vital to success overall.

For the counter-insurgent the provision of security, material benefits and good government for the population is not enough: the population has to be induced to give its free consent to the government – and in Algeria this was not given. In fact it was withdrawn. In part this was the result of the unbridgeable divide in Algeria on racial and religious lines, in part by the fact that because of the international situation and the presence outside Algeria of considerable insurgent forces, intact and undefeated, there could be no inducement for the population to support the French

effort. But in large part the alienation of Algerian society stemmed from the methods used by the French. Though the insurgents used barbarous methods to terrorize the population – the lopping off of ears, noses, lips, mutilation generally and macabre methods of inflicting death – the French counter-measures, particularly in Algiers, totally polarized society. On the French figures, one in eight prisoners taken in for questioning in Algiers in the first six months of 1957 failed to survive interrogation. Torture became widespread: the war a competition in terror. Not only was this self-defeating in terms of the Moslem population, it was inimical to the interests of the French state itself. French society, disillusioned by losses and effort not simply in Algeria but before that in Indo-China, would not countenance the use of such methods on the part of a democratic and civilized society. Nor would it, in the last resort, admit the claim by extremist elements in the French Army to the effect that the total effort needed in Algeria determined the Army's involvement in and, if necessary, domination over, domestic politics, if the government of the day seemed to fail in its duty (as interpreted by them). Most of the French Army rejected such a notion but it was sufficiently widely held to help bring down the IVth Republic in 1958. The doctrine of *La Guerre Revolutionnaire* seemed to reverse Clausewitz's dictum that war is an instrument of policy, and to assert that politics exist to serve a total war effort. As it was, the success of French tactics made such a concept a very potent force until de Gaulle secured the ascendancy of

the French state over the army by purging many army units and, finally, by granting independence to Algeria.

For counter-insurgents the only known method of combatting insurgency, rural and urban, lies in the basic methods that worked so well in Malaya, even though in fighting that campaign the counter-insurgents possessed many advantages that others have not enjoyed. The basis of political success in Malaya was intensive policing and extremely high quality Special Branch action, of military success the superiority of the security forces in minor tactics – intensive patrolling, marksmanship, ambush and anti-ambush drills. Essential to victory in Malaya was the close co-ordination of army and police actions within the framework of civilian control and the rule of law. One must recognize, however, that in certain cases the priority must be on orthodox military actions, such as in a situation where insurgent forces operate in strength in conventional fighting (such as the situation in South Vietnam when the Americans began to deploy in strength in 1965). But in the final analysis, granted that revolutionary warfare is total war, the military effort is secondary and the essential characteristics are political; in this situation the military can handle no more than part of the conflict. The essential struggle is for the control and loyalty of the population and in this economic, social, educational, health and welfare programmes and the evolution of meaningful political programmes are more important in the long run than the security situation, although these ideas cannot take root in a society where security is under stress.

The Superpowers Line Up

Soviet soldiers double down a range in Hungary during a live firing exercise in the early spring of 1967.

The dropping of atomic bombs on Japan in August 1945 was a testimonial to American industrial and technological might. On all the seas ran the writ of the American Navy; in the air her aircraft were in numbers and quality infinitely superior to those of any other nation; on the ground her armies were numerous, lavish in equipment and experience. The only power that could be realistically contrasted to her was the USSR but she was markedly inferior industrially, economically and financially. Moreover, American superiority over the Soviet Union in two other fields was most notable. Firstly, the USA had a monopoly, and then decisive superiority, in nuclear weapons; secondly, she was geographically superior in that while both countries had an extension of power and influence during the course of the war, the American expansion had been to a point where she (or her allies) surrounded the USSR and possessed the means of taking a future fight to the Soviet homeland while remaining invulnerable herself. These considerations dominated strategy for nearly two decades.

With peace came American demobilization, but as the Cold War assumed its shape in the form of disputes over Germany, communist backing of the Greek Civil War, the Czechoslovakian coup, the Korean war, it fell upon the Americans to assume the leadership of democracy since they alone possessed the resources and the capacity for leadership needed to resist the aggressive nature of Soviet dictatorship. The Europeans were manifestly incapable of defending themselves since Britain and France had colonial commitments and the West Germans were disarmed. The formation of NATO in 1949 and the formulation of the Lisbon goals in the 1950s were unable to rectify this weakness. For the first years NATO was utterly dependent on the American nuclear umbrella for protection. American strategy was relatively straightforward, and was based on deterrence whereby they undertook immediate nuclear retaliation against the Soviet homeland in the event of Soviet aggression. The aim of American policy was to ensure such damage to the Soviet state through the razing of her cities that any political objective sought by the Soviets could count for very little if anything when set against the devastation of the homeland. And such was American power and certainty of intent that this strategy was very effective.

Initially the strategy of American deterrence was placed on air power – the simplest, cheapest and for a long time the only means of delivering a nuclear weapon on its target. But technology, just as it had produced the nuclear bomb, was working to produce other means of delivery of such bombs and, moreover, that technology was not the monopoly of the Americans any more; the Soviets were working along the same lines, though at later dates. These two factors led to an evolution in the strategy of nuclear deterrence. Although the US/NATO basic strategy did not change, the means by which the strategy was to be implemented underwent fundamental alteration. Because of the danger of placing total reliance on a single weapons system (the aircraft carried nuclear weapon) the search began for alternative means of delivery. These alternatives have become embodied in the triad system which is a combination of aircraft (both large strategic bombers and carrier-borne aircraft with gravity bombs and stand-off missiles), strategic missiles from submarines, and missiles fired from land bases, either mobile or especially protected in hardened silos. The missiles themselves evolved from single warhead weapons into missiles carrying different numbers of warheads, some pre-set to land in a group around a target, others capable of independent targetting. These developments ensured a multiplicity of weapons and a diversity of delivery that meant that an enemy could not hope to launch a surprise attack that would eliminate all the nuclear weapons of his opponent. The ability to withstand such a strike against one's own nuclear forces and still retain sufficient power to inflict unacceptable damage on the aggressor – termed a 'second-strike capability' – is a vital pre-requisite of deterrence strategy. In this process the role of land-based nuclear forces remains vital, even though the main element of the triad system remains with the submarine-launched ballistic missiles.

Because of these developments, and because the development of a Soviet nuclear deterrent seemed in the late fifties and early sixties to bring to an end American nuclear invulnerability, there was a movement away from the concept of deterrence based on massive retaliation. Given the power of the nuclear arsenals there was always the possibility that the reliance on nuclear weapons would make the Americans, muscle-bound by forcing a choice between surrender or suicide, gain only posthumous revenge. Thus one had in the early sixties the evolution of the idea of flexible response as the deterrence strategy for NATO. In this, the Americans envisaged NATO attempting to fight conventionally in the event of Soviet aggression in order to try to find

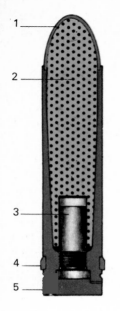

HESH
1. Outer nose casing of
   aluminium or copper
2. RDX plastic explosive
3. Base fuse
4. Driving band
5. Fixing screws

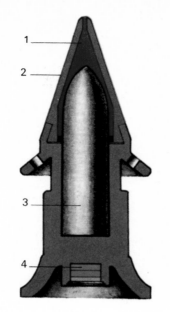

German APCR
For Tapered Bore
1. Phenolic plastic filling
2. Aluminium alloy ballistic cap
3. Tungsten carbide core
4. Tracer composition

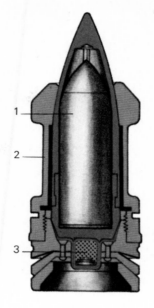

APDS
1. Armour-piercing core of
   tungsten carbide
2. Plastic or light mangesium
   alloy sleeve or sabot
3. High-explosive charge

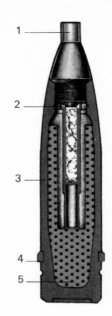

High Explosive
1. Nose cap
2. Fuse assembly
3. Outer casing
4. Driving band
5. High explosive filling

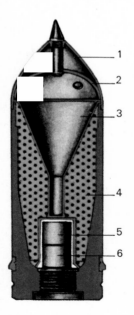

HEAT
1. Nose cap
2. Diaphragm
3. Steel liner
4. PEN/D1 charge
5. Exploder charge
6. Tracer

Armour Piercing
1. Solid shot
2. High explosive charge
3. Detonator
4. Driving band
5. Fuse assembly

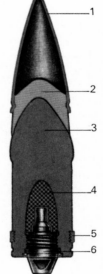

Armour-Piercing Capped
(Improving AP shell)
1. Nose cap
2. Casing
3. High explosive charge
4. Driving band

APC + Ballistic Cap
1. Windshield
2. Cap
3. Body
4. High explosive charge
5. Driving band
6. Brass fuse and tracer

Scorpions of the 17th/21st Lancers and the 14th/20th
King's Hussars during Exercise 'Glory Hawk' – the
first major Scorpion exercise to be held in Germany.

ways of resolving the conflict without recourse to
nuclear release on a strategic level. Given that both of
the superpowers in the sixties were edging their way
towards a situation of mutually assured destruction in
the event of nuclear exchange – and the destruction of
everything on earth at the same time – this change was
essential.

The problem for NATO was that such a policy,
while perfectly sensible for the Americans, spelt ruin for
the Europeans. The buying of time by fighting conventionally would have to be achieved in fighting in
Europe – on the territory of NATO. This was likely to
be extremely destructive indeed. For the Europeans
only a policy of massive deterrence made sense. Moreover, if such a policy of flexible response was to be put
into effect, it could only be achieved at the cost of a
considerable increase in the size of conventional forces.
In the event of massive retaliation, conventional forces
were limited in that their main role was designed
to demonstrate a willingness to defend by the presence
of some strength on the ground, rather than to be seen
as a means of prolonged or successful defence. Therefore more ground forces needed to be deployed, but the
immediate tactical problem was the manner in which
these should be used. The basic choice was for forces to
be deployed forward or to the rear. The advantage of a
deployment to the rear was that while an initial assault
would hit air, the defender would be able to discover
the main line(s) of enemy effort before battle was
joined, and if necessary, redeploy before contact. Such
tactics would also have the advantage of forcing the
enemy to come on to chosen ground and to have tired
himself and his supplies in the process. In fighting this
type of battle the enemy could be channelled into 'killing zones' which he would have to pass through in order
to continue the advance and could be attacked there by
armour, artillery or infantry (or any combination of the
three) or by tactical nuclear weapons. Politically, however, the notion of a rear defence – possibly involving
defence on a distant but major natural feature – was not
really acceptable to a country that was the scene of such
intended action. For the 'host' country defence must
involve the forward defence of territory, not ceding
voluntarily ground that in any case could be used as
negotiation counters should conflict be limited or contained. The tactical disadvantage of such deployment,
on the other hand, is the exposure to the full shock of
the initial assault and the possibility of mistaking the
main axes of advance by the enemy. An initial strategic

deployment forward could prove impossible to rectify
if it was proved to be wrong.

For the USSR conventional forces have played a very
different role than those in the west. An ability to overrun western Europe by virtue of superior conventional
strength was the essence of Soviet deterrence strategy
when she lacked nuclear weapons and when she was
decidedly inferior in such weapons to the United States.
The value of these conventional forces, however, has
greatly risen as a result of the Soviet achievement of
nuclear parity with the United States (or if not parity
then something approaching it): the continued Soviet
build-up of strength on land, sea and in the air can only
be seen in the light of this situation. While it is true that
obsolescence of design, the demands of new technology and the peculiar defence requirements of a
country so vast as the Soviet Union can be used to explain away the immense growth in armed strength in the
last decade, the present stance of Soviet forces, ground
troops included, can only be seen in the strategic context whereby the communist bloc seeks to secure such a
strategic superiority over the West that the latter would
be denied any means of effective response in some future
crisis. At the last congress of the CPSU Foreign Min-
ister Gromyko made just this point.

In the purely military sense, by reason of its political
ideology, the strategy of the Soviet Army is committed
to the offensive, the chief characteristics of this stance
being the emphasis on speed and mass. Speed is of the
essence since Marxist ideology dictates the ultimate
victory of the economically more powerful combatant.
Given the marked industrial inferiority of the communist bloc to the West the Soviets must be committed
to a rapid campaign of conquest before the resources
of the West can be fully mobilized. Mass, the
other characteristic, has long been the hallmark of
Soviet operations but in the last few years there have
been qualitative and quantitative increases in Soviet
formations that give new dimensions to the meaning of
mass, certainly within the context of the Central Front
in Europe. As a result of the Soviet invasion of Czechoslovakia in 1968, the number of Soviet divisions in
eastern Europe (excluding the Soviet Union) rose from
twenty-six to thirty-one: since 1973–74 the firepower of
these divisions has risen by about 20 per cent. The increase in firepower largely stems from the fact that the
anticipated (or desired) speed of advance envisaged by
the Soviets in the early sixties led to the introduction of
self-propelled artillery since towed guns could not be

The new NATO FH70 during troop trials on Salisbury Plain. The gun developed jointly by the Germans, Italians and British has its own power unit for local redeployment. A German crew (far right) move the gun, while Italian gunners ready the ammunition and check the alignment. Cooperation on arms development not only saves money and speeds construction, but also ensures standardization throughout NATO.

relied upon for rapid and adequate fire support in fluid situations. Unfortunately for the Soviets no self-propelled guns were available to meet this requirement, and this led to the employment of old tanks, the T54/55, being used in this role. As self-propelled artillery they were allocated as an independent unit within Motor Rifle Divisions; these independent units have not been phased out with the subsequent introduction of the self-propelled artillery.

Soviet ground forces are formed into three types, depending on the predominant arm: the Motor Rifle Division, the Tank Division and the Parachute Division. All are, in fact, all-arms formations with indigenous infantry, armour, artillery and specialist troops with supporting arms and lines of communication formations. The airborne forces are the elite of the Army and consist of seven divisions. These can be used either in small formations for reconnaissance and sabotage or in larger formations, size depending on the state of the air battle and the nature of the objective. In the latter role they are likely to be employed in the seizure of bridges and river crossing sites by parachute

or helicopter-borne landings. The brunt of the land fighting, however, would obviously fall on the Tank Divisions (sixteen in Eastern Europe and forty-nine overall) and on the Motor Rifle Divisions (fifteen and 110 respectively). Both types of division are formed on a 3:1 ratio, with the Motor Rifle Division having its independent tank battalion left over from its SP artillery role. At all levels from division to battalion, the units have their own organic combat support arms which overall contributed to a massive concentration of firepower, particularly of the artillery. Overall a Tank Division deploys 325 tanks and about 9300 men: a Motor Rifle Division 266 tanks and 11,600 men. The artillery support differs between the divisions in that the Tank Divisions rely on their own guns for anti-tank protection whereas the Motor Rifle troops are given a battalion of anti-tank artillery. Overall the divisions are organized into either Tank or Combined Arms Armies on a 3:1 basis, though occasionally there may be more than four divisions in an Army. The Armies are then organized into fronts.

Basic Soviet practice has not changed substantially

An ammunition crew member runs back for the next shell as a German crew fire the FH70 at Larkhill in England. British gunners have fired on ranges in Sardinia and joint NATO exercises have been held in different host countries in Europe. This cooperation enables armies to compare notes on standard operational procedures and familiarize themselves with the terrain they might one day be called to fight over.

since the war though their capacity to wage deep offensive warfare has naturally increased with the rapid mechanization of the Soviet Army. Emphasis is placed on mobility, the concentration of force at a given place in the attack, surprise, aggressive action and a desire to close with the enemy and retain contact until his destruction is complete. In order to ensure both width and depth to an attack, stress is laid on extensive operations (witness the 1944 offensive), and close co-ordination between units with air support. The aim of such operations is either the encirclement and hence annihilation of the enemy forces or the deep penetration of the enemy positions in order to destroy his supplies, reinforcements and capacity to fight. To achieve such objectives the Soviets aim to make a decisive breakthrough by concentration of decisive numerical and material superiority at a point of their choosing (usually taken off the map). This would entail a division formed into all-arms battle groups (armour predominating) on a front no more than five miles wide with either one, but preferably two, axes of advance. In all likelihood a division would be given only one axis of attack on a frontage of no more than two miles. Given the fact that an army frontage would be between twenty and thirty miles and that a division in the assault would be between thirty and sixty miles in depth in order to avoid bunching and hence nuclear attack, the flanks would in effect be left open. Reconnaissance elements would be used not simply in front of the leading elements but on these flanks and between the divisions that comprise an Army. In the assault the Soviets would normally attack in two echelons with the first echelon being the more powerful. This would contain a majority of the armour and be supported by all the artillery. The task of the first echelon would be to break through the enemy front with the second echelon passing through the (probably exhausted and possibly shattered) first echelons in order to exploit the breach and maintain the momentum of the advance. By the same token second echelon divisions would pass through the first wave in order to press on to objectives, or to make a breach if this proved beyond the capacity of the leading divisions.

The concentration of manpower and vehicles (over 2500 in a Motor Rifle Division) is obviously very hazardous and complicated, especially in the tactical switch from line of column advance to a rapid lateral deployment for an attack once contact is made. To this end the advance is led by a divisional recce element some thirty miles ahead of the regimental recce

elements that would be some five miles in front of the vanguard. The vanguard would usually be a motor rifle company and a tank platoon. In a sense all three have a similar role in that they are intended to locate, assess and report the enemy's positions and, where possible, to overcome them and continue the advance. This would enable the division to avoid having to waste time in deploying for a set piece assault. In the assault, the leading regimental battlegroup would deploy into battalion battlegroups, two forward, one in reserve, with the artillery in close support some three miles from the enemy positions. The task of the artillery is to provide covering fire during the deployment into companies and hence into platoons as the actual assault is taking place. (This deployment naturally is intended to take place beyond the effective range of infantry weapons.) The assault is intended to be carried through at speed, ideally with APCs and not with dismounted infantry; when the infantry are forced to put in an attack on foot the APCs are intended to provide covering heavy machine-gun fire.

Set piece battles are not favoured by Soviet forces, particularly since they could involve attacks on strong positions (including hull-down tanks) and would need time and superiority of numbers which a commander would not necessarily have at his disposal. More favoured is what is known as 'the encounter battle' which involves an open action by a Soviet formation against an enemy moving for the counter-attack. In essence it is a 'fire and manoeuvre' situation on a large scale but it is favoured by the Soviets because in this case the enemy would be robbed of his natural defensive advantages and Soviet superiority of numbers could be employed to maximum effect. The encounter battle envisages a major flanking movement after reconnaissance elements and the vanguard, acting as the pivot for the deployment, have blocked the course of an enemy advance and pinned him, hopefully at the same time discovering the size and direction of advance of the enemy. Depending on the ground deployment, the main attacking force would go to the flank while the enemy was held in his position and prevented from preparing defensive positions. The flanking movement is intended to envelope the enemy position until, under artillery cover, the attack is pressed home in regimental strength. Because of the danger of the flanking movement itself being taken in its flank, the Soviets envisage using defensive arrangements – such as the deployment of AT guns, ATGW helicopters and minefields – to hold their position from attack. The obvious problem of such an attack is the one inherent in any battle – success cannot be guaranteed and the role of attacker and victim can be reversed.

Perhaps the most frequently practised Soviet exercise is one of the more difficult operations in war – the forcing of a river obstacle in the presence of an enemy. Since any advance by Soviet forces into western Europe would result in their encountering a major water obstacle, it can be seen why this is of great concern. In theory they regard such attacks as routine, considering that they should be carried out from the line of advance without any delays either in forcing the obstacle or in breaking out of an established bridgehead. Accordingly they have equipped themselves with extensive and efficient amphibious and engineering equipment. All but one of their APCs – and that an obsolete one – are amphibious, as is the PT 76 light reconnaissance tank. Soviet MBTs can, given a hard river bottom and shallow banks, snorkel while their bridging and ferrying equipment has proved useful for the Indians in the war for Bangladesh, and for the Egyptians in the 1973 war with Israel. Nevertheless there may well be a difference between intention and reality since fitting snorkels is a time-consuming process and some delay in reconnaissance, organization of the crossing and in re-organization after it is only to be expected.

The problems of mounting a river assault are numerous, not least the prospect of having to select crossing sites without the advantage of previous reconnaissance. There is also the problem of mounting attacks on a relatively narrow front but not bunched so closely that a nuclear attack would be invited. Emphasis is placed on opportunist crossings by reconnaissance groups, which would attempt to seize and hold unprotected crossing points. But for a deliberate assault engineer reconnaissance would be necessary some time before the arrival of the main body. In a divisional assault the forward unit – usually a motor rifle battalion battlegroup – would be moved forward in order to clear the approaches to the river, take positions on the far bank and, if possible, prevent an enemy counter-attack or withdrawal. The division itself would cross in two echelons, the stronger part being the second to cross. That they reverse their normal procedure of advancing with the stronger part of their forces forward suggests that a river crossing may not be so routine after all, but the reason for holding the major part of strength back for

the second wave is the belief that the second echelon would be able to maintain the momentum of the advance by passing through the first wave without having to re-organize. In the first echelon assault, the leading regiment would normally commit two or three battalions, each with all three companies deployed forward in line, ideally all entering the water together. On reaching the far bank the infantry dismount from their APCs in order to secure immediate objectives. Once the leading battalions have secured the far bank – and the leading regiments could have immediate objectives as far as six miles beyond the river itself – the second echelon is moved forward with GSP ferries and bridging equipment in order to take over the armour. Tanks are not committed in the first echelon. The time reckoned to elapse between the first assault and the tanks crossing is about thirty minutes. To aid the process, airborne forces could be used either to secure the crossing before the arrival of the division or during the actual assault. Close air support generally is envisaged for the assault and for the period of the immediate re-organization in the bridgehead when the leading motor rifle units would be lacking their armour and artillery support. General artillery support would be available, up to and including nuclear release, if the objective was considered sufficiently important. It could be that for a river assault crossing, the Soviets would use their rocket artillery against enemy positions and that chemical weapons would be used extensively, since these would give area saturation. Smoke would be used extensively to cover the attack during all initial stages.

The set-piece battle, the encounter battle and river assault are the basic stock-in-trade tactics of the Soviet Army: simple, direct and not very elaborate or sophisticated, they play directly to the strengths of the military machine. In outline the methods to which the Soviets are committed tend towards the expanding torrent concept on a totally mechanized scale and up-dated to incorporate new weapons. A major source of weakness may lie in supply and maintenance, both of which are rather poor and here the Soviets could encounter severe problems. The Arab-Israeli war of 1973 revealed the high rates of ammunition and equipment expenditure on the modern battlefield. They were somewhat hidden in the 1967 war by the early impact of Israeli air power and the disorganization of the Arabs. In 1967 the Israelis crushed the Egyptians, Jordanians and Syrians with contemptuous ease. In the euphoria of victory the Israelis and many outside observers tended

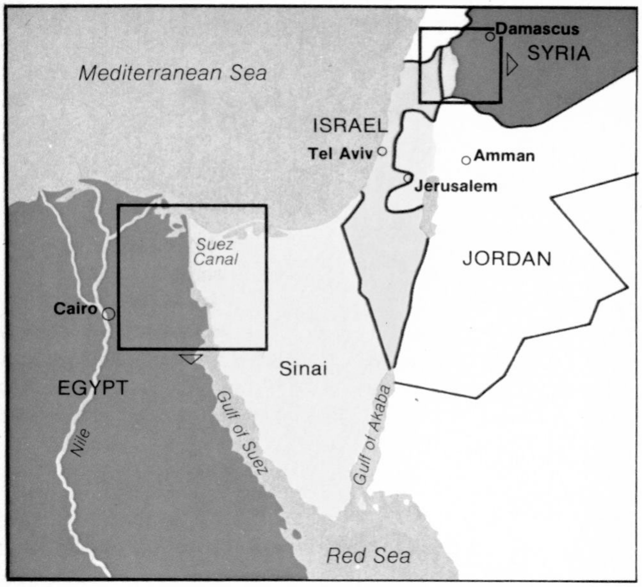
Damascus
SYRIA
Mediterranean Sea
ISRAEL
Tel Aviv
Amman
Jerusalem
Suez Canal
JORDAN
Cairo
Sinai
EGYPT
Nile
Gulf of Suez
Gulf of Akaba
Red Sea

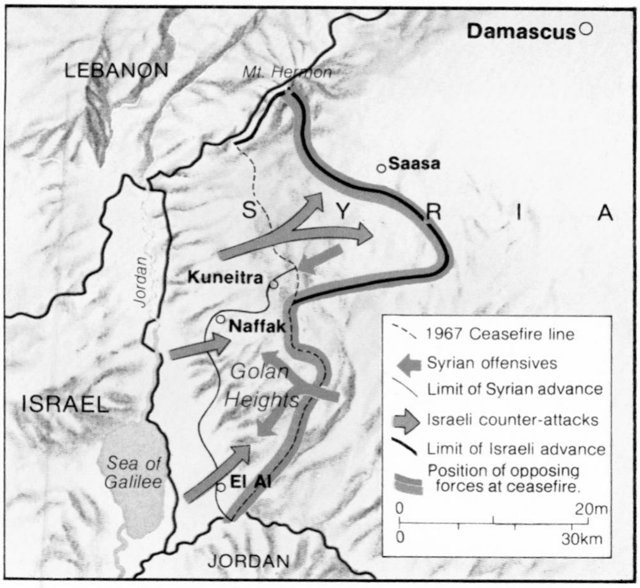
Damascus
LEBANON
Mt. Hermon
Saasa
S Y R I A
Jordan
Kuneitra
Naffak
Golan Heights
ISRAEL
Sea of Galilee
El Al
JORDAN
1967 Ceasefire line
Syrian offensives
Limit of Syrian advance
Israeli counter-attacks
Limit of Israeli advance
Position of opposing forces at ceasefire.
0 20m
0 30km

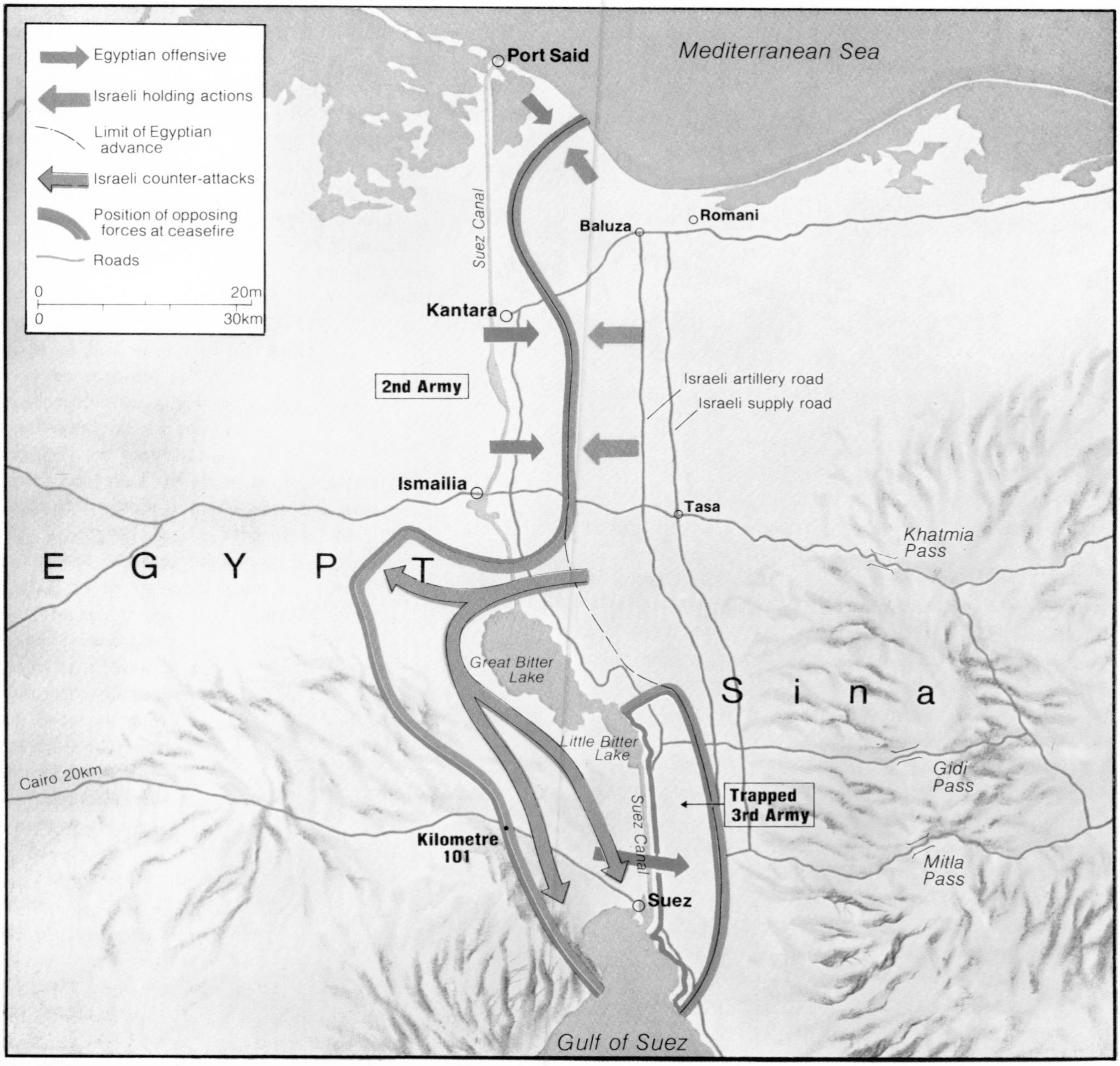
Egyptian offensive
Israeli holding actions
Limit of Egyptian advance
Israeli counter-attacks
Position of opposing forces at ceasefire
Roads
0 20m
0 30km
Port Said
Mediterranean Sea
Suez Canal
Baluza
Romani
Kantara
2nd Army
Israeli artillery road
Israeli supply road
Ismailia
Tasa
Khatmia Pass
E G Y P T
Great Bitter Lake
S i n a
Little Bitter Lake
Gidi Pass
Cairo 20km
Trapped 3rd Army
Kilometre 101
Suez Canal
Mitla Pass
Suez
Gulf of Suez